Cognitive Behavioral Therapy

An Essential CBT Guide to Rewiring the Brain and Overcoming Anxiety, Depression, and Intrusive Thoughts Using a Highly Effective Form of Psychotherapy

Contents

Introduction

Cognitive behavioral therapy (CBT) is a form of therapy that focuses on the connection between your thoughts (cognitive) and your actions (behaviors). CBT works based on the concept that your thoughts about various circumstances stimulate how you feel emotionally and physically towards those circumstances. In most cases, these feelings are neutral or positive; however, they can also be negative and destructive. For those experiences, CBT seeks to use the power of cognitive restructuring and behavioral implementation to support you in experiencing freedom from your destructive feelings and behaviors.

CBT was originally proposed in the 1960s by Dr. Aaron T. Beck, who was a psychiatrist at the University of Pennsylvania. Dr. Beck studied and practiced psychoanalysis and had conducted several tests on the psychoanalytic of patients who were suffering from depression. He was surprised when all his original beliefs around depression were invalidated by his findings which ultimately lead him to look even further into the way depression could be conceptualized. What he found was that patients who have depression experience streams of negative thoughts that arise spontaneously within their minds. Dr. Beck called these cognitions "automatic thoughts." From there, he went on to discover ways to begin evaluating these automatic thoughts and coached his patients through thought-based practices that were used to combat the automatic thoughts and restore peace within the brain. This went on to become what we know as cognitive behavioral therapy.

CBT is an evidence-based psychological treatment that works on the foundation of thoughts and behaviors. This is not about "thinking positive so that you can feel better". CBT is about strategically adjusting your thought processes so that you can adjust the way you feel about things; thus, helping you have less intense responses to the world around you. It works in a very specific manner and requires consistent implementation for it to be effective in helping you treat your behavioral concerns such as anxiety, depression, PTSD, anger, and even procrastination. It has even been used to treat eating disorders and various addictive behaviors in people.

Based on research, CBT has been proven to be just as effective, if not more effective, than using medication alone when it comes to treating depression and anxiety specifically. People who experience these two psychological disorders are known to experience consistent relapses in their depressive or anxious episodes even if they are being treated with specific medications. When these individuals partake in CBT, however, they are far less likely to relapse and, if they do, they are far more resilient towards their relapses. This means that if you experience depression and you use CBT to treat it, you are less likely to experience major depressive episodes following successful treatment because you are now equipped with the proper skills to overcome depression before it becomes problematic.

If you are ready to begin living a life free of the problematic symptoms of your anxiety or depression, "Cognitive Behavioral Therapy" will show you everything that you need to know to understand CBT and begin implementing it in your own life. Be sure to take your time and read this book in the order that it has been written to successfully treat yourself with CBT. Make sure that you truly find the time to fully understand the tools in Chapter 4 and that you understand how to implement them before moving forward so that you are equipped to deal with any challenges that may arise along your journey. This will ensure that you are ready to embrace the entire journey and are successful in your efforts.

Part 1: Clarifying the Problem and Setting Goals

Chapter 1: Identifying the Problem

You think more than 70,000 thoughts every single day. Your thoughts are a constructive tool developed by your mind to support you in interpreting the world around you, making sense of what is happening, and interpreting events taking place in your environment. The number of thoughts that you experience in a day is so high that you likely don't even realize that you are actively thinking most of the time. While you experience it happening, you are most likely not staying consciously aware of your thoughts processes and patterns and what they are telling you.

As someone who is seeking to experience healing within your mind, it is important that you realize that your thoughts are not factual statements regarding the world around you or the events that are taking place. Instead, they are merely interpretations. The reality is that your thoughts are actually electro-chemical impulses that take place within your brain. This means that the thoughts and emotions that you experience in response to the world around you are not factual representations of the world around you but instead representations of your *perception* of the world around you. For example, if you were in an environment that was dark and had few people around, you might interpret that environment to be a dangerous place. However, if the environment were, in fact, safe, then the only reason it would be considered "dangerous" is that you have perceived it to be that way, not because it actually is. What you *think about* something is the foundation upon which emotions are created, not what that something *actually is*.

How each individual person thinks about the world around them and what emotions arise from various experiences or situations depends on many different factors. Things such as your previous experiences, your culture, your upbringing, any religious beliefs that you might have, and your family's values all impact how you interpret the world around you. Because of this, not everyone is going to interpret the world in the same way. If you were to take two people from different backgrounds and put them together in the same environment, the chances are they would each have completely different emotional responses to the world around them.

The reality that thoughts are not factual and that we all experience different thoughts and emotions in relation to our environment proves that we cannot assume that everything is exactly as we believe it to be. In doing so, we may wrongly interpret our environment and behave in a way that is completely inappropriate to the said environment. This either causes us to create a negative experience between ourselves and someone else or simply within ourselves. For example, if you were to enter an environment that you perceived as unwelcoming, you might be rude or withdrawn from others in that environment and find yourself feeling extremely uncomfortable and struggling to create connections with others. Alternatively, you might find yourself experiencing intense anxiety or discomfort because your belief of the environment has you feeling as though you are unwelcome, even if you truly are welcomed and wanted.

Know that your thoughts are not always factual and that means you do not have to believe them immediately. Instead, you can challenge your thoughts and look for opportunities to identify the truth so that you can respond to your environment as it is; thus, giving you the opportunity to respond in a way that is more appropriate to your actual situation. To begin challenging your thoughts and creating the opportunity to experience freedom from your perception so that you can see into the truth, you need to know how to identify the problem, i.e., your negative thought patterns. By identifying negative thought patterns or unwanted emotional responses, you can begin to create a plan to take back control over your thoughts and experience greater emotional freedom in the process.

Automatic Thoughts

Automatic thoughts happen in response to the world around us, hence the name. When you experience an automatic thought, you will likely experience it in a way that brings an image, memory, or words into your mind in a fairly instantaneous manner. You may also experience a physical sensation, an imagined sound, or even just a deep knowingness about something that takes place in your intuition. Because automatic thoughts happen in such an unconscious way, we rarely take the time to slow down and critique these thoughts to discover if they are actually true or not. We rarely question their validity, so we find ourselves completely believing the thoughts as they are. This means that if you have an automatic thought about something, you will probably believe it no matter how obscene it may truly be. For example, if someone cut you off when you were driving, and in your mind, you labeled them as something harsh, you may automatically believe that to be true. In reality, it may just be someone who is in a rush to get to work or even to the hospital, and they are not actually an unkind person at all, they are just in a hurry.

There is rarely an experience that happens beforehand that makes you consciously aware of your automatic thoughts. They simply pop into your head, rattle around for a while, and pop back out so that a new one can take their place. These thoughts are typically presented to you by your subconscious mind and support you in interpreting the world around you exactly as you believe it to be based on your previous experiences or knowledge you have from elsewhere. Because these thoughts are automatic and typically rooted in previous experiences, we have a tendency of feeling as though we are being personally victimized by our thoughts when "bad" things happen. For example, if you were raised to believe that not making your bed every morning was a horrible thing and you forgot to make your bed one morning, you might end up experiencing automatic thoughts that say something like "I'm a bad person!"

Since you automatically believe these thoughts, this can lead to them becoming destructive and harmful. They become even more destructive and harmful when your automatic thoughts become habitual and persistent, repeating themselves over and over in your mind and leading you to believe them even further. They can even set off an entirely new chain of thoughts that can be negative as well, particularly if the original, believable thought was negative, too. Your thoughts will continue to follow these habitual, automatic themes for days, weeks, months, years, or even decades, leading to you having an automatic thought pattern that is either constructive or destructive.

Based on the nature of automatic thoughts, these are believed to be the foundation upon which our core beliefs are based on. After a lengthy period of time, repeating the same belief to yourself over and over again, it essentially becomes programmed into who you are and leads to you having this core belief lingering in the background of your life. Core beliefs can further shape your experience, interpretation, and perceived environment and either supports you in having a positive experience or a negative experience. Once you have something wired into you as a core belief, it requires a stronger strategy to eliminate that belief. This is where CBT comes in. By helping you identify where the belief came from and shaped your thoughts, you can develop a new core belief that is more productive to your positive life experiences.

Intrusive Thoughts

Intrusive thoughts are unwanted thoughts or images that arise in your mind to produce a disturbing or distressing experience for you. They are a form of automatic thoughts that can become destructive in nature. Often, intrusive thoughts are obsessive, and we find ourselves automatically thinking them repeatedly; thus, producing the distressing or disturbing feelings on a consistent basis. An example of an intrusive thought would be, *I am worthless, no one loves me*. When you think something like this, especially on a regular or obsessive basis, it can result in you developing a core belief that you are worthless and that no one will love you. As a result, you may find yourself acting compulsively to try and cope with the painful feelings or emotions that are arising from these unwanted thoughts.

Although they can be rather terrifying, intrusive thoughts are not factual representations of the truth. Just because you experience intrusive thoughts does not mean that the material within them is true. It also does not mean that somewhere within you, there is a desire to act upon the information being presented to you in your thoughts. For example, a common intrusive thought that people have involves driving into a crowd of people when they are driving their car. Realistically, if you have this thought, you likely have zero desire to drive into a crowd of people. So, naturally experiencing a thought like this can bring about many disturbing or distressing feelings. You may begin to wonder what is wrong with you, why you are feeling that way, or if you have some secret dark place inside of you that longs to cause harm unto others. However, the truth is actually quite the opposite. This is a classic case of intrusive thinking, and the thoughts do not reflect what you want to do, but instead are likely a reflection of what you do not want to do. Your mind simply thinks of the most inappropriate thing it can imagine that you do not want to experience and then produces a thought based on that inappropriate thing.

The more you try to push intrusive thoughts out of your mind, the more you may actually have these thoughts. Research done at Harvard University showed that the harder people tried to stop thinking about something, the more they actually thought about it. This happens because as you attempt to not think about the said thing, your mind will try to "check in" to see if you have truly stopped thinking about it. As a result of this "check-in", the thought comes back and you experience it again; thus, recreating the experiences of distress and disturbance.

Intrusive thoughts are normal, but they can create a serious disturbance in the mental wellness of people who experience them on a regular basis. In fact, intrusive thoughts are common in things like depression, anxiety, PTSD, and even more serious cases of anger. If you experience intrusive thoughts and feel as though you have no control over them, you might find yourself feeling as though you are trapped inside of a mind that is scary and even dangerous. This fear can lead to you feeling an even deeper experience of anxiety, depression, PTSD, or anger. What you need to do is use CBT to begin regaining control over your thoughts and putting an end to the intrusive thoughts that you have been experiencing so far. Luckily for you, the tools needed to help you do that are provided in this book.

Identifying Your Thought Patterns

Before you can begin healing your thoughts, you need to have an idea of what it is that you are trying to heal. You need to identify what thought patterns you are having, how they are causing troubles for you, and where they are coming from. When you understand your own thought patterns in this way, it becomes easier for you to develop a clear path for how you can begin healing your thoughts and designing a more positive and empowering life for yourself.

In cognitive behavioral therapy, there is a very simple and straightforward tool when it comes to identifying your thought patterns and discovering how they are contributing to your negative experiences. The tool that you will use is called "Thought Record". A thought record is essentially a sheet of paper or a journal where you jot down a few notes each time you consciously become aware of a negative thinking pattern you have been experiencing, such as intrusive thoughts. By using this Thought Record, you can begin to get to the root of all the negative thoughts that you are having. The chances are, you will recognize a pattern (or multiple patterns) in your negative thinking that will support you in making sense of what your triggers are when it comes to having negative thought patterns. For example, maybe, any time you are around a person wearing a black toque, a negative thought creeps in because of a negative experience you had with a person in a black toque. The pattern, then, would revolve around people who are wearing black toques and the emotional response that you have when you witness them.

You can easily create your own thought record by using a journal or a blank piece of paper and creating a space for you to write down each of the seven pieces of information every time you experience a negative thought:

- Where were you? (Write down where you were, what you were doing, and who was with you.)
- Emotion or feeling (Write down the emotions that described how you were feeling and rate the emotions from 0-100 wherein 100 means you felt the maximum level of the said emotion.)
- Negative automatic thought (What was the negative thought(s) going through your mind at the time? Did they trigger any memories or images in your mind?)
- Evidence that supports the thought (What evidence leads you to believe that these thoughts were true?)
- Evidence that does not support the thought (What evidence can you find that leads you to believe that these thoughts were false or inaccurate?)
- Alternative thought (What alternative thought could you think of instead of the intrusive thought?)

- Emotion or feeling (What did it made you feel after critically thinking about your experience?)

You want to track your thoughts for several days to get a strong sense of what your thought patterns are and how they are affecting your emotional wellbeing. Ideally, you should practice using your thought record on a daily basis for at least seven days. Using it longer will support you in having a stronger idea of all your patterns and how they are impacting you. The thought record itself will also support you in demystifying your thoughts and finding healthier ways of thinking about the situations that you are experiencing. This can be a great way to begin the process of healing your mind from negative thought processes.

Types of Negative Thoughts

You have learned about automatic and intrusive thoughts, but you might be surprised to learn that there are nine different types of negative thoughts that people tend to experience. Below are included each of these negative thought types and what they mean so that you can begin identifying what types of negative thinking you are experiencing the most. Having a stronger understanding of what these thoughts are can be helpful in determining whether or not they are true and what types of alternative thoughts you can turn to in order to experience freedom from your negative thoughts.

All-Or-Nothing Thoughts

When you feel as though things need to be done perfectly, or else they are a complete failure, you are experiencing an all-or-nothing thought. These thoughts lead to a very black-and-white way of thinking and, more often than not, lead to you feeling as though you cannot do anything right because small amounts of negativity feel like a complete loss to you. For example, if you give a presentation and not everyone loves it, you will feel as though you were a failure even though this is not true. All-or-nothing thoughts are a very common experience for those who find themselves identifying as "perfectionists".

Catastrophizing

Any time you believe that the absolute worst possible thing is going to happen, you are catastrophizing. Often, catastrophizing thoughts can lead to stress, anxiety, depression, and other ailments because they lead to you automatically believing in the worst possible things. For example, if you think of something like "if I leave my house and walk down the street, I will get hit by a car and die," you are catastrophizing.

Emotional Reasoning

If you experience a feeling and then believe that it must be true because you feel that way, you are experiencing emotional reasoning. The emotional reasoning sounds like this: "I feel unloved; therefore, I am unloved." This is a common type of negative thought that can quickly reinforce your feelings and lead to you genuinely believing that everything you feel is based on factual truth.

Filtering

Filtering is a negative thought process whereby you disregard the positive in favor of the negative. For example, if you take a test and you score 90%, but instead of celebrating your score, you stress over the fact that you must not know 10% of the content. This means you are filtering. Essentially, you are filtering out your positive experiences in favor of your negative ones.

Jumping to Conclusions

Any time you assume that you know something based on a small piece of evidence you have, you are jumping to conclusions. For example, if you walk into work one morning and your boss does not smile at you like they normally do, you assume they're angry with you. This is clearly showing you are jumping to conclusions. Realistically, many other potential factors might lead to the lack of smiling, such as if they were busy, thinking, or upset from something that happened earlier that morning. Your assumption is a symptom of you jumping to conclusions.

Mind Reading

If you feel as though you know what someone else is thinking without ever having actually been granted the evidence supporting your belief, you are practicing a negative thought process known as mind reading. Mind reading sounds like this: "I know that person does not like me, I can feel it." This is often following a situation where very little, if anything, happened to prove that the other person did not actually like you. Instead, you are attempting to read their mind and formulate facts based on your thoughts and feelings.

Overgeneralizing

When you experience something in one or two instances and then claim that it happens every time, you are experiencing a negative thought process known as overgeneralizing. Overgeneralizing can be extremely negative because it stops you from recalling positive experiences in your life. An example of overgeneralizing something is if you were to say, "No one ever respects me."

Personalizing

Personalizing is a form of negative thinking whereby you assume responsibility for everything you experience or witness. For example, if your best friend does not message you back, you may feel as though you did something wrong to result in them being angry with you. In reality, they may have just been busy and unable to message you back, and you did not do anything wrong.

Should Statements

"Should statements" refer to you having a specific expectation as to how things "should" be. For example, if you believe that there is a specific way to clean the dishes and you say something like "I should know how to clean the dishes properly" yet you missed something that you believe *should* be done, you are thinking negatively. These types of thoughts typically hold you up to unreasonable standards and make you feel poorly when you do not achieve them, even if your reason for not achieving them was completely valid.

Chapter 2: Setting Your Therapy Goals

CBT is a forward-focused approach that relies on setting goals and focusing on how you can improve your future. Unlike other forms of therapy that rely heavily on talking about and healing the past, CBT focuses on the present moment and how you can adjust your thought processes to improve your future experiences. Part of being able to successfully make that happen is having a goal in mind. Setting goals ensures that you have something to look forward to that is both measurable and achievable. Ideally, these goals need to be meaningful too so that you are genuinely invested in doing your part to make sure they come true.

There is a very specific way in which goals are going to support you with your CBT, which means that you need to be fairly specific in your goal setting. In this chapter, we are going to explore how you can set achievable goals for yourself so that your therapy can be both effective and efficient. Make sure that you take the time to genuinely invest in this practice as it is equally vital to your success as any other step in this book. Identifying your goal will support you in determining what your course of action needs to be to support your success. This chapter will walk you through the process of setting the perfect goals for your therapy so that you can move forward in your healing journey with clarity and direction.

Identify Your Goal

The first thing you want to do when it comes to setting your goal for CBT is to identify exactly what it is that you want to achieve. An easy way to start is to simply ask yourself, "What is my overall goal?" This will give you an idea of what it is that you desire to achieve and what exactly you are trying to move away from. By keeping things simple and staying focused on results, you will ensure that your therapy is efficient and successful.

As you set your goal, focus on making one that is positive and forward thinking. Remember, any time you attempt to move away from something such as a thought, you attract it into your life more because your brain will regularly check in to see how you are doing. If you want to move away from a certain behavior, you need to choose a positive solution-focused goal rather than a negative problem-focused goal. For example, you do not want your goal to be "to stop feeling so anxious" because this focuses on trying to move away from something you don't want anymore. Instead, you want your goal to say "to start feeling more peaceful and confident" as this focuses on a positive solution that heals your trouble with anxiety without having such an emphasis on anxiety itself.

You also want to make sure that the goals you are setting are "SMART". SMART goals are highly achievable because they include all of the components required to create a strong and clear goal that has measurable results. To set a SMART goal, you need to ensure that it has the following qualities:

- *Specific*

It is important that you be highly specific in the goal that you are setting when it comes to setting goals for yourself. You need to know *exactly* what you are working toward so that you know what you need to do to get there. Being specific ensures that you are not driving aimlessly looking for a destination that was never actually specified. Imagine driving around your city attempting to find your friend's house when they had not yet given you the address. It would be frustrating, right? Instead, it would be made much simpler if you had the address and a map that showed you how to get there. The same goes for your goals. When you are specific about the destination, making the plan to get there becomes much simpler.

An example of a specific goal when it comes to CBT would be "to feel confident in situations involving my family". If you were someone who felt intensely anxious around your family, this would specify that you want to feel more confident around them so that you can stop experiencing anxiety. Plus, it is written in a positive solution-oriented manner that keeps you focusing on what you want as opposed to what you don't want.

- *Measurable*

Making your goal measurable ensures that you can take sizeable steps towards your goal and have a clear understanding as to whether or not they are getting you the results that you desire. In the aforementioned goal, the measurable quality was the feeling of "confidence". If you experience anxiety around your family and you desire to feel confident, then you know that you need to pay attention to how confident you are feeling each time you go around them. If you find yourself feeling less anxious but not yet feeling confident, you know that you need to adjust your approach or take bigger action in achieving your desired results.

- *Achievable*

It is important that you do not infuse your goal with an all-or-nothing negative thinking process. You do not want to set a goal that requires you to change your personality completely and become an entirely different character. Instead, you want to choose a goal that is genuinely achievable so that you do not feel as though you are constantly chasing something that will never come your way. Be reasonable with yourself and your expectations and avoid trying to set your standards too high. This doesn't mean that you can't expect more from yourself, but it does mean that you shouldn't expect an unreasonable amount.

Setting goals that are unachievable are common for people who have frequent negative thought processes. The subconscious thoughts surrounding this thought process are, *If I set the goal so high, I can't achieve it and then I can continue feeling bad about myself.* This may sound harsh of your brain, partly because it is, but also because you may not want to believe that your brain would want to sabotage you. The truth is, your brain does not want to sabotage you at all; what it is trying to do is protect you by keeping your core beliefs reinforced with evidence. The process of breaking down core beliefs can be emotionally trying at times as it requires you to discard your beliefs about what is "right" so that you can see things for what they are. In an attempt to avoid you from enduring this, and to save its own energy, your brain tries to sabotage you to keep everything "normal".

- *Relevant*

The goals you choose should always be in alignment with the issue that you are trying to overcome. With setting goals for CBT, you want to make sure that you choose a goal that directly reflects the reason why you have sought after this information in the first place. Upon purchasing this book, what was the very thought you had? What was it that you hoped to change and overcome? This thought likely reflects the challenges that you are currently facing. Therefore, it should be considered when you are setting your goals. Keeping your goals focused on something that is relevant is important as it ensures that what you are focused on truly matters to you.

If you are unsure as to what truly means the most to you right now and what part of your thoughts need to be addressed, check back to your thought record log. Consider what the most prominent pattern on your record is and start there as this is likely the one that is holding everything else back. Starting at the very foundation of everything that needs to be adjusted is the best way to make sure that you are going to have the strongest impact when it comes to genuinely changing your life with CBT.

- *Timely*

Finally, the goal that you officially choose needs to be a timely goal that you are actually capable of working towards achieving at this moment. You do not want to attempt to set out to change something when you are not presently in a position where you can. Fortunately, most thought changes come from within, so they are almost always going to work out with your timing. However, sometimes you may find that it is not necessarily the best time to work on a certain pattern so you may choose to start somewhere else. For example, if you are attempting to overcome anxiety around your family but there is presently someone who is ill in your family, thus causing more stress between you and your relatives, it may be a better idea to wait until things have settled down before you begin.

Alternatively, you might set a more reasonable time frame for yourself when it comes to considering how much success you want to have achieved by a specific time. Rather than expecting yourself to be completely confident in three months, for example, you might give yourself six. Be honest with yourself and focus on adjusting things that you truly can approach at this time in your life so that you are not setting yourself up for failure by trying to climb a mountain before you are ready.

Identify Your Starting Point

Now that you have a SMART goal in place, it is time to start mapping your course to success! The first thing that you need to do is identify what your starting point is. To determine your starting point, you need to honestly assess where you are at in your life regarding this current goal. An example is expanding on the previous goal. If you want to be more confident around your family but you currently experience crippling anxiety every time you even think about calling them, you need to be honest about that. Rather than determining that your starting point will include you strutting into their homes and standing tall as you defend yourself against all of their remarks, determine your starting point as growing more confident with simply talking on the phone with them. This is more reasonable and achievable and honors where you are at in your life right now.

If you are not entirely sure as to where your starting point should be, consider journaling about where you are at right now. Take inventory of everything going on in your life relating to this specific area of focus and be honest about how it impacts both you and your ability to achieve your desired goals. Spend some time really exploring all areas of your life from friends and family to your personal emotions and thoughts and honestly account for how your goal is being impacted by all of these areas of your life. This is going to help give you a more realistic account of what your exact starting point is so that you can chart a course that is going to genuinely account for you and your needs.

Remember, this is a private experience that is unique to you, so there is no need for you to attempt to glorify where you are currently at. If you are having a particularly challenging time, honestly embrace that and allow yourself to honor where you are at without feeling the need to pretend that you are further ahead. Being more honest with yourself will support you in having a more positive experience by allowing you to start with steps that are manageable and achievable for you at this time in your life.

Identify the Steps

Once you have identified both your goal and your starting point, you need to determine what the necessary steps are for you to succeed. Since you are working towards achieving a stronger and more positive thinking behavior, it is important that you keep your steps manageable. When it comes to overcoming things such as anxiety, depression, anger, or any other troubling experience, you need to give yourself space to genuinely process your emotions. Attempting to process too much at once may result in you feeling overwhelmed and struggling to move forward as a result of emotional exhaustion. Give yourself time to adjust and heal your emotions in addition to healing your thought patterns so that you can fully embrace each step and move forward with a strong foundation.

To create strong and manageable steps, you need to chunk your goal down into smaller portions. How this looks will depend on what goal you are trying to achieve, but ultimately, you want to be able to turn these chunks into their own mini goals. That way, each time you achieve one step towards your larger goal, you are achieving a goal in and of itself. This supports your mind in experiencing the gratification it desires and keeps you focused on moving forward. If you find that certain steps are harder than others or they are not getting you the results you desire, you can easily adjust those steps to help keep you on track.

In addition to charting out your steps, consider obstacles that you may face along the way and how they may impact your ability to succeed in achieving your goal. With something as sensitive as emotions, facing unexpected obstacles can be overwhelming and can slow you down. Considering what obstacles you may face and accommodating for them, planning for them, or at least preparing for them, is going to support you in confidently moving towards your goal even if you face a challenge. Mentally, this is going to prevent you from feeling distraught, doubtful, or defeated any time you face a challenge because you will already be prepared to endure anything that said challenge might bring your way.

Once you have considered what the smaller portions of the goals are, you need to lay your steps out in order. Write them down from start to finish as if you are writing out a game plan to get you from point A to point B so that you can clearly see what it is that you need to do. This will ensure that you are putting one foot in front of the other and not attempting to bite off more than you can chew at any given time.

Get Started

Finally, all you need to do is get started! If you successfully followed the steps above, then your goal should be perfectly set up so that all you need to do is embark on the first step in your plan. Give yourself the pep talk you need to get started and then go ahead and begin taking action!

Part 2: CBT Techniques

Chapter 3: CBT Techniques for Specific Ailments

Using CBT to approach your healing can look different depending on what it is that you are attempting to heal from. For example, healing from depression and healing from anger will look completely different. Knowing how CBT looks for each unique ailment can support you in fully recovering from them through this therapy practice. In this chapter, we are going to cover CBT techniques for the following ailments: anxiety, PTSD, depression, anger, and procrastination.

Keep in mind that if you are dealing with various ailments at once, you will want to address each of these. How you choose to address multiple ailments will ultimately be up to you. Check in with yourself and ask which solution feels best. Is it to slowly heal each ailment at once or to heal them one at a time starting with the one that causes the most problems for you? Following the path that feels best for you will ensure that you are not overwhelming yourself and that you are experiencing complete healing from each ailment that you have been struggling with.

CBT Techniques for Overcoming Anxiety

As you focus on overcoming anxiety, you need to focus on overcoming all that comes along with anxiety, too. This means that you need to practice building up your tolerance towards uncertainty, your ability to recognize rumination (repetitive worrying thoughts,) your ability to recognize thought distortion, and your capacity to increase your mindfulness. You will also want to begin building up the ability to speak kindly to yourself and tolerate your imperfections without feeling as though they take away from who you are and what you have to offer the world.

The best way to create your action plan with CBT is to consider your thought records and begin determining what thoughts are contributing to your anxiety and what behaviors are arising as a result of these thoughts. The way you think has a massive impact on the development of your anxiety. For example, if you were invited to go out to coffee with someone new, your thoughts would completely shape the experience for yourself. If you were to think of this as a fun new opportunity to make a connection, you might feel happy and excited by the idea. If you were to think that coffee wasn't really your thing or you weren't overly interested in the said person, you might feel neutral about the idea. If you were to think about how you struggle to make conversation with new people and that you will probably make a fool of yourself in front of this new person, you would find yourself feeling anxious and sad about the experience. Each thought process and emotion would lead to a completely different behavioral reaction in the people around you. For this reason, you have to be very conscious of your thought processes and how they might be contributing to the development of your anxiety.

With anxiety, you need to practice "thought challenging" or critically assessing your thoughts to determine whether or not they have any validity. You can do this by first identifying what the negative thought is, and then challenging it by analyzing the evidence upon which it is founded and where it comes from. You might also look for opportunities to weigh the pros and cons of your thoughts to see if they are genuinely helping you or if they are hindering you from trying new things. Once you have successfully done that, you can begin replacing your negative thoughts with realistic thoughts. Note, the key here is not necessarily to replace them with "positive" thinking, but instead, replace your negative thoughts with realistic thinking. For example, the coffee date *could* go badly, but it could also be incredible, and you could have a great time. By adjusting your perspective, you can introduce new thoughts and expand your mind so that you can begin exploring and experiencing a more positive mindset and emotions in your life.

Another great practice when it comes to overcoming anxiety with CBT is using exposure therapy. Exposure therapy essentially states that you are going to expose yourself to situations that make you anxious with the conscious awareness that anxiety will arise. Through that awareness, you can intentionally adjust your thought process to accommodate a new perspective that is less likely to produce anxious feelings. After exposing yourself to your triggers enough times, you begin to realize that your trigger is not nearly as fearsome as you believed it was and you no longer experience such immense anxiety towards it.

CBT Techniques for Overcoming PTSD

Individuals with PTSD experience similar symptoms as those who experience anxiety, except that PTSD is more intense and long-lasting. Whereas anxiety tends to come in waves and then disappear, PTSD can affect individuals on an ongoing basis with no seeming end to the symptoms. Often, people with PTSD find themselves feeling trapped in their trauma and struggling to discover any solace or comfort from the distress that has been caused by traumas. As a result, the thoughts of someone with PTSD tend to be more frequently interrupted by disturbing and distressing thoughts than someone who has anxiety.

If you are living with PTSD and you are searching for an opportunity to overcome your symptoms and experience freedom from your distress, there are some key CBT techniques that you can practice to help you overcome your traumatic responses. As you use CBT to overcome your PTSD, you will need to re-evaluate your thought processes, identify your distortions and assumptions, and balance your thought processes to release catastrophizing and other negative thought patterns from your mind. You will also need to expose yourself to your inner narrative related to your trauma so that you can begin to experience desensitization towards the memories themselves and maintain a higher sense of control when these memories or triggers arise. Another great way to support the healing of PTSD with CBT is to educate yourself on how trauma changes your brain so that you can have an educated evidence-based approach to changing your thoughts. Sometimes, knowing exactly what is happening in your brain to cause your symptoms of PTSD can be extremely helpful in helping you realize that what you are experiencing through your thoughts are symptoms and not facts.

As you begin to develop the techniques to overcome your PTSD, you will need to monitor your thought record and consistently update it to keep a close eye on how you are progressing. This will also support you in discovering where your triggers lie and what exactly you need to begin desensitizing yourself towards. Furthermore, you can begin educating yourself on these triggers and retroactively replacing your thoughts (which were based on your distorted perception) with facts. For example, if your PTSD was triggered by someone yelling in your general vicinity, you may immediately begin experiencing flashbacks and fear that result in other symptoms arising. You may find that later, on that night, you could not rest, and sleep seemed impossible. When you finally did fall asleep, you had nightmares. This is because your brain subconsciously perceived the yelling as a direct threat to you.

Now, you can retroactively evaluate the experience and assure yourself that you were not being attacked and that you were completely safe in that experience. You can also support this reassurance with evidence from the environment, i.e., by recalling that said person was not yelling at you, or maybe, they were not yelling at all, but instead, they were cheering in celebration. This will help you begin to retrain your mind to see things in a more accurate and factual manner so that your subconscious can stop feeling the need to instantly protect itself any time someone raises their voice. You want to practice this reflection for every single trigger that you experience. Consistently reassure yourself that you are safe and that the experience you had was safe even if it didn't feel like it to you. In doing so, you teach your mind to begin seeing a new perspective in these experiences so that you can begin feeling more peaceful each time they arise.

CBT Techniques for Overcoming Depression

For many people, depression arises after the repetitive thinking of negative thoughts that feature a lack of hope, motivation, or inspiration. In many cases, these thoughts are harmful and destructive and are often worded in a way that tears the sufferer down, thereby causing them to feel as though they are worthless and that they do not have anything to offer the world around them. This can result in a negative spiral that can either lead to depression or worsen depression that might be caused by other conditions, such as hormonal imbalances.

If you are experiencing depression, you need to use CBT in a way that addresses your negative thoughts and improves your self-talk. Instead of obsessing over your shortcomings and emphasizing your flaws through obsessive thinking, you need to begin swapping these thoughts out for more realistic ones that are rich with compassion and consideration. Your thoughts need to become more gentle and considerate towards yourself if you are going to improve your depression through CBT.

The most common technique used in treating depression with CBT is swapping your thoughts. This works by first identifying the negative thought that is causing you to feel depressed or that is increasing your depression, and then swapping it out for a more positive or realistic thought that can support you in improving your mood. You will do this by learning to identify your thought patterns automatically and recognize when you are experiencing thoughts that are unhelpful. For example, say you wake up one morning, and your first thought is, *This day already sucks. I don't see any point in even trying. I already know I am not good enough.* This thought is unproductive and will only worsen the way you feel about yourself and about life in general. Through thought swapping, you can recognize that this was an unhelpful thought and swap it out for one that is more productive. An alternative thought might be something such as, *That thought is not helpful. I know I can make an effort and at least try. I am worth the effort. Let me start by getting out of bed.* Then, you would continue to take it one step at a time and swap your thoughts out every single time you notice that they are unproductive. After doing this often enough, your mind will begin to recognize the more positive perspective and naturally start swapping your negative thoughts out for these realistic ones that nurture positivity. As a result, you will begin to feel more positive.

Even though you are recognizing them on a more consistent basis, you should still continue to write them down in your thought records to ensure that you are truly improving your depression in a positive manner. This also gives you the opportunity to see where your most common thought patterns lie and what they reveal about the actual cause of your depression. For example, if you find that you are consistently experiencing negative thoughts in relation to your self-worth based on what one of your parents told you when you were growing up, you can guess that the cause of your depression is childhood related. This allows you to focus on healing these childhood wounds by using evidence from your adult life that supports true reality versus the reality that you interpreted as a child. For example, if your parents consistently told you that you were poor at making or keeping friends, you may now feel as though you are not worthy of having friends in your life. You can challenge these thoughts by recognizing that you are no longer a child, you were likely never truly bad at making friends, that your parent may have been projecting on you, and that they likely had a hard time showing true love or acceptance. This helps you realize that what your parent said was not necessarily true and gives you the space to recreate your own reality now, as an adult.

CBT Techniques for Overcoming Anger

Anger is commonly considered to be a secondary emotion because it tends to arise when other emotions are not being adequately handled. For example, if you are experiencing anxiety or fear and you are not producing an "answer" for these emotions, you may then begin to experience anger. This anger is meant to give you the energy and focus required to develop a solution for overcoming the anxiety or fear that you were originally experiencing.

Some people grow up without any clear guidance or direction on how they should express or respond to emotions that they experience in their life. As a result, they frequently struggle to manage their emotions in a productive manner, which can lead to consistent feelings of anger and frustration. It is likely that this anger arises from both the fear of not having their emotional needs met, as well as from the habit of responding to things with anger due to knowing that the emotional need will not be fulfilled otherwise. Anger is also frequently aroused from the negative thoughtform of "should thoughts". For individuals struggling with anger, CBT is a great way to retrain their mind to approach situations with emotions other than anger while still successfully having their needs met.

For CBT to be effective in treating anger, you will need to discover what your triggers are and begin developing resistance towards those triggers. You will also need to develop trust in yourself and your ability to get your needs met in a productive manner so that you can stop relying on anger to fuel the process. This requires you to prepare for angry events by determining what it is that you want to do the next time you are angry, such as approaching it with a more level-headed response. Then, when you encounter an angry experience, you need to identify the pain-point, or the emotion being triggered, swap out your "hot thoughts", and respond to the anger itself. You can do this by addressing the anger within you, recognizing its purpose, and then choosing to fulfill that purpose in a less aggressive manner. And then, you need to disengage from the aggression and discover a way to respond to the event itself with a more level-headed approach.

This process for addressing anger will be used on a regular basis in order to be effective since problematic anger is typically a habitual behavioral pattern. By regularly processing anger in a more constructive manner, you can begin to break this habit and enforce new ones that support you in getting your needs met without causing harm to anyone else or yourself. If you find that you deeply struggle with anger, you may need to expose yourself to lesser triggers first so that you can begin building up your response system in a less intense environment. You should also keep a detailed thought record of each angry encounter (including the ones you handle effectively) so that you can remain clear on what arouses your anger and, if necessary, heal that part of you that feels so angry or neglected.

CBT Techniques for Overcoming Procrastination

Procrastination is typically the symptom of a more challenging inner experience, although not always. For some people, procrastination arises because they fear that they cannot perform well enough, so they simply avoid performing at all. For example, if you fear that you cannot do well with a work assignment, you may procrastinate doing it because you worry that you will not do well enough and that you will somehow suffer because of it. Procrastination can also arise from things like boredom, disinterest, or feeling adversity towards the action itself. In some cases, a small amount of procrastination is not necessarily problematic and may even be normal. However, when procrastination begins to interfere with your world, social life, and your confidence in yourself, it is time to address your procrastination and begin overcoming it.

When it comes to overcoming procrastination, you need to build up stronger confidence in your abilities, adjust your perspective of the situation you are facing, and get very clear on what your outcome needs to be. By doing these three things, you can begin feeling the inner motivation you need to accomplish things while also developing the outer motivation by increasing your desire to achieve whatever it is that you have set out to achieve.

The best way to begin changing the way your mind works around procrastination is to begin identifying small goals and setting out to accomplish them. This is going to support you in exposing yourself to situations that typically trigger procrastination, while also building up your inner rewards system. Each time you identify a small goal and achieve that goal, you teach yourself what you need to do to curb procrastination and actually keep yourself motivated. Then, when the goal is achieved, your brain releases dopamine which causes you to feel good. This is like a mental reward as dopamine creates a strong positive reaction in your brain that leaves you feeling almost as though you are experiencing the 'happiness high'. The more you condition yourself to create this reaction in your brain, the easier it becomes for you to motivate yourself and stay focused on achieving your goals.

When it comes to finding ways to combat your procrastination, you will need to emphasize your focus on challenging your thoughts. Often, procrastination is experienced when we justify why we can put an activity or action off until a later time. For example, *I can watch TV for half an hour and then start my task later. Half an hour isn't much time, so I will still have plenty of time to get it done.* Before you know it, you have justified your way out of time, and you no longer have time to waste. Then, you feel an intense amount of stress and get overwhelmed as you attempt to get a significant amount of work done with not enough time left to complete the task. When you see these thoughts arising, you must challenge them and begin backing them up with evidence that supports your need to get the task done. For example, *The last time I decided to watch TV for half an hour, it became three hours and then I did not have enough time. I need to start now so that I can be done. Then, if I have time left, I will watch some TV after.* This more rational thought process realistically explores what will happen if you do not get the task done and supports you in getting up to get it done.

Chapter 4: Tools Used in CBT

Creating your CBT healing pathway starts by identifying your goal and then determining what thought patterns need to be treated, such as those relating to anxiety or anger. Then, you need to equip yourself with knowledge of the tools that are available to you to be used in CBT. With the understanding of what tools are available to you, you can begin creating the foundation upon which your healing will happen. This chapter will explain what CBT tools and techniques are used in virtually every form of therapy. You will want to read through these tools and develop a strong understanding around them, and then rely on this chapter as a resource when you encounter a bout of negative thinking.

It is important that you understand that these tools are based on your mind; therefore, it may seem challenging or even overwhelming to attempt to enforce them all at once. The goal with CBT is never to make all of your changes immediately and expect them to stick overnight. Instead, it is to equip yourself with the correct resources and continue making small yet powerful changes so that your response to triggers continually improves over time. The more you reference this chapter and educate yourself on how these tools work, the easier you will find it to employ these tools during situations where you need to adjust a negative thinking pattern. Over time, the habitual thoughts that lead to you struggling on an emotional level will begin changing in favor of the new habits that you are introducing into your life. This is how you will know that the tools are working. You can track your progress and change using your thought records as a way to get a strong understanding of how you are improving and what may need to be adjusted to support you in achieving your goals.

Journaling

Journaling is a common tool used in therapy to support individuals in feeling a sense of release from their thoughts and emotions. When you journal, you allow yourself to openly and freely express everything that you are feeling inside and explore what may be causing these feelings. You can write about everything from the trigger to your reaction and how you feel after the fact. Journaling is also a great way to reflect on parts of your life that may be responsible for producing triggers in the first place. In general, journaling is a great practice to use when it comes to therapy as it supports you in releasing your thoughts and feelings from your mind and getting them out in front of you. This can be very therapeutic.

Using a journal is especially important with CBT because it works not only as a tool to help you release what you feel inside but also as a tool to support you in getting a deeper understanding of yourself and what you need. Journaling after an episode of difficult emotion/s allows you to freely and openly write exactly what you are feeling and then later reflect on that and get a sense of what caused the experience. Through this understanding, you can then begin implementing the proper adjustments into your life so that you can prevent it from happening again, or at least reduce the amount in which it happens.

Journaling is also going to help you get an idea of how far you have come, what is working and what isn't, and what may be a good solution going forward. As you reflect on what you have written, you can visually see your progress on paper which can support you in feeling as though your hard work is paying off. There are many valuable benefits to journaling as you are undergoing CBT.

It is important that you use journaling diligently in your CBT practices. Ideally, you should journal at least once per day, and any time you have experienced an episode of difficult or troubling emotion/s. Any time your anxiety, depression, anger, PTSD, or procrastination tendencies arise, use this as an opportunity to write down what happened, what you did in response to that experience, and what the result was. This can be used as your thought record or, in addition to your thought record, a way to keep track of your episodes and get a stronger and deeper understanding of what may be going on for you each time a trigger is pulled.

Unraveling Cognitive Distortions

Cognitive distortion is the name used to describe the process of your brain lying to you or producing thoughts that are false. For example, if you are experiencing anxiety and you believe that you are dying because your heart rate has quickened, you are experiencing a cognitive distortion. The primary goal of CBT is to unravel cognitive distortions so that you can begin experiencing stronger control over your thoughts so that you no longer experience the spiral that comes from these distortions. By gaining control over them, you can recover control over yourself entirely and prevent or slow down the progression of the symptoms of your emotional troubles, such as depression and anxiety.

Unraveling your cognitive distortions requires you first to develop an awareness of what distortions you are vulnerable to and how they impact you. Typically, cognitive distortions are a part of your automatic and intrusive thought processes, and they tend to slip in under your conscious radar. The best way to bring them forward into your awareness consciousness is to begin taking notice of the times you experience the symptoms of your emotional ailment. Once you recognize your emotional state, you can begin considering what your current thoughts are, what your thoughts were when it first started, and what your thoughts were right before it started. This gives you an understanding of the progression of your thoughts and emotions and how they resulted in you experiencing emotional symptoms of your thought patterns.

Having the negative thought list from Chapter 2 can be extremely helpful in supporting you in identifying what negative thinking patterns you are experiencing and the aftermath of those patterns. Then, after you have identified your negative thought pattern, you can move on to the process of cognitive restructuring.

Cognitive Restructuring

Cognitive restructuring is the process of challenging your negative thought patterns and cognitive distortions and replacing them with realistic and factual thoughts that essentially combat the distortion. The cognitive restructuring process takes place over three steps: identifying what caused the distortion, challenging the distortion, and replacing it with realistic information. Typically, cognitive restructuring is used to restructure actual beliefs that have taken root in your mind and resulted in you feeling bad about yourself. For example, you have a belief that if you have no money, you are worth nothing. Then, every time you look in your savings account, you see that you have not saved up any money yet because your budget is typically spent paying your bills and keeping a roof over your head. Because of your belief, any time you look in your savings account, you would believe that you were worthless, and this would only be changed if you were able to add more money into your savings account. The reality is that everyone is born worthy and that money does not change your value, but your belief holds you back from believing so. As a result, you may never believe that you are worth anything and you may continue feeling too depressed to make any changes in your life.

Instead of allowing faulty beliefs to reinforce your negative or unwanted emotions, you need to challenge them and replace them with new beliefs that are realistic and manageable. You need to rethink what your beliefs are and how they are negatively impacting you and can be adjusted to actually serve you in feeling better about yourself and the world around you. For example, if you were to challenge the belief about money and choose to believe that everyone is inherently valuable simply for being born into existence, you would realize that your belief about money is no longer valid. This adjustment in your belief allows you to begin feeling better about yourself and can improve your mood enough that you then have the energy required to increase the funds in your savings account.

The best way to change your beliefs is to challenge them. To challenge your beliefs, you need to question why they exist and where they come from so that you can have a strong understanding as to why you believe them in the first place. Often, we find that our beliefs come from something someone said to us many years ago. This is typical during our childhood or early adulthood. They can also be developed by hearing the same thing being repeated to you by someone in your life. You then automatically learn to believe these beliefs and never take the time to consider whether they are constructive or destructive and if they are actually supporting you in living a better life or not. In the instances where they are not, you need to question why you have held onto them and what they may be protecting by sticking around. In most cases, you may realize that they are not actually protecting anything and have no value. You simply continued to believe them because you always have. Then, you can choose a new belief and replace your old beliefs with said new belief; thus, fulfilling the technique of cognitive restructuring.

Exposure and Response Prevention

Exposure and response prevention are techniques commonly used in people who have the obsessive-compulsive disorder (OCD); although it can also be used in other situations. With exposure and response prevention, you want to repeatedly expose yourself to a trigger that typically stimulates a compulsive behavior or response from you. For example, if you compulsively bite your nails every time someone yells at you or around you, you want to expose yourself to loud environments and consciously refrain from biting your nails. Once you are done, or during the process, you can write about how you are feeling and what emotions were triggered for you as you attempted to deny the compulsive response.

The idea behind exposure and response prevention is that the more you consciously enter situations that typically arouse a compulsive response out of you, the more you can consciously hold back from engaging in the compulsive behavior. Over time, you will have exposed yourself and held back from the behavior so many times that you no longer experience the intense need to engage in the compulsive behaviors, so you no longer have to worry about the triggers.

If you are using exposure and response prevention on something more intensive, such as compulsive behaviors that could be perceived as harmful to yourself or someone else, it is important that you do so with the support of someone else. Dipping into these types of emotions and compulsions on your own can be scary, so it is important that you feel as though you have adequate support in helping you overcome these experiences successfully. You also want to make sure that you are fully mentally prepared to handle the experience so that you do not feel as though you are being blindsided by the compulsions as they arise.

Interoceptive Exposure

If you struggle with anxiety, interoceptive exposure is a tool that you will need to take advantage of. Interoceptive exposure requires you to expose yourself to feared sensations in order to elicit the anxious response. Then, you activate the unhelpful beliefs that are associated with the sensation and allow yourself to facilitate new learning about the experience so that you can adjust your perspective on it. The idea of interoceptive exposure is to educate you on how your symptoms of panic are not dangerous even if they feel uncomfortable or worrisome.

An example of interoceptive exposure would be if you were afraid of bees and wasps and you put yourself in the vicinity of them to elicit the fearful response. Then, as you are in their presence and the fear begins to arise, you recall information about bees and wasps that remind you about how positive they are to the environment and about how unlikely it is that you would be stung by one. As you continue to remain in their vicinity and allow the fear to run its course, while reminding yourself of the education you have learned about bees as wasps, you begin to overcome the panic and find yourself feeling less stressed out in the presence of them. The same goes for anything else that may elicit panic attacks within you. By consciously arousing the panic, you allow yourself to adjust the internal narrative around it and reduce the panic that you experience as a result.

Nightmare Exposure and Rescripting

Nightmares, especially ones relating to traumas, can be particularly disturbing and can lead to many distressing emotions if they occur on a frequent basis. Nightmares are a common symptom in people who have experienced traumas or who are experiencing intense negative emotions on a consistent basis. Nightmare exposure and rescripting work similarly to interoceptive exposure, except for the specific thing that you are trying to arouse, which are the emotions relating to the nightmares.

To arouse the feelings you experience in your nightmares, you must first begin to recall them in as much detail as you can. As you do, the emotions accompanying the nightmares should begin to arise once more, typically overcoming you sometimes in a rather intense manner. With these emotions now stirred up once again, you can identify what emotion you would rather experience and develop a new image associated with your desired emotion. After moving back and forth through the process of awakening the emotions relating to the nightmares and then rescripting them with new desired emotions and images, you train your mind to adjust its focus each time the nightmare is aroused. Typically, what will end up happening during your sleep then is that, if the nightmare begins to start, your mind will naturally switch to the preferred emotion and image that you have rescripted it with. As a result, you should no longer experience disturbing nightmares.

Note that when you are dealing with a nightmare, rescripting it can take time since nightmares themselves typically happen when you are asleep; therefore, it can be challenging to tap into them with your conscious mind. You might need to continually use the rescripting method for several nights before you find complete freedom from your nightmares. If you do not experience instant relief, you need to continue practicing your rescripting process until the nightmares begin to go away. Trust that as long as you stay committed, they will disappear in due time, and you will no longer have the disturbing or distressing experience of your nightmares.

Playing the Script Until the End

People who suffer fear or anxiety often find themselves getting trapped in the worry of the worst-case scenario and the pain that would accompany it if it should happen. Due to their fear of the pain, they find themselves struggling to move forward or take action on anything because they fear that they will experience that pain. In many cases, the fear can lead to panic or anxiety because they are so worried about what the pain will be like and what they could lose or what might happen to them. So, they remain frozen in fear.

If you find yourself getting caught in the worrying narrative of fear and pain associated with the worst-case scenario when your anxiety or panic triggers are pulled, playing the script out to the end may be the perfect tool for you to call on. All you have to do with this tool is to consider the part of the narrative that you are feeling stuck on and then ask yourself, "And then what happens next?" This can help you put your worry into perspective and realize that, in many cases, the worst-case scenario is truly not a big deal.

For example, if the stuck-thought that you are experiencing is, *If I speak in front of that crowd, I will make a mistake, and they will tease me. It will be horrible*, then you may stay trapped in the fear of making a mistake. This can make the idea of getting on stage frightening and may even hold you back from going and speaking altogether. However, if you were to follow that thought with the question "And then what happens next?", you might realize that the worst-case scenario truly wouldn't be as horrible as you might think. For example, maybe your speech goes horribly, and people don't enjoy it, but the chances are that they completely forget about it by the time the next speaker is done speaking. Or, maybe they do remember it, and they get a good laugh from it while you gain a positive learning experience so that you can do a better job next time. In most circumstances, the worst-case scenario is truly not the "life or death" experience that our panic makes it out to be. By playing the script out until the end, you can support yourself in realizing that, in most cases, not everything is as bad as it may seem.

Progressive Muscle Relaxation (PMR)

Progressive muscle relaxation or PMR is a process where you relax one group of muscles at a time until your entire body is relaxed. In people who experience panic or anxiety, PMR is a great way to mindfully bring relaxation back into the body in a holistic manner with a manageable approach. Attempting to completely relax all at once in the face of fear or panic can be nearly impossible as anyone who has ever experienced panic would know. You simply cannot encourage your entire body to relax at once and expect anything to happen. It is too much for any one person to attempt to do all at once. If anything, you may attempt to consciously try and then your lack of positive results will lead to you feeling even worse and wondering why you cannot relax.

With PMR, you consciously focus all your attention on just one area of your body at a time. During this process, you allow the muscles in your area of focus to completely relax, and you consciously and intentionally release any stress or tension that may be residing within that part of your body. Then, when that one area is completely relaxed, you move on to the next one. In doing so, you allow yourself the opportunity to completely relax each area of your body until your entire body is relaxed from any panic or tension that you may be experiencing. Because you have broken the process up into manageable stages, your ability to stay focused and completely relaxed is improved, and you are more likely to experience full relief from your anxiety.

Relaxed Breathing

Relaxed breathing is not necessarily a CBT-specific tool, but it is regularly incorporated into CBT to support individuals in experiencing complete release from their emotional symptoms. Relaxed breathing is a mindfulness practice that is used to help draw relaxation into your body through the breath so that you can restore rational thinking to your mind during particularly emotional experiences. As a result, you can critically consider your thoughts and begin using cognitive restructuring to slow the progression of your problematic thoughts and troubling emotions.

When you are experiencing emotional distress, your body begins to change the way your automatic nervous system functions. Your breathing changes, your pulse changes, your muscles tense or weaken, and you begin to feel completely different within your body. The idea is that you can slow down or even reverse these symptoms by intentionally controlling your breathing; thus, pressuring the rest of your system to slow down and even out. From this more relaxed state, you can experience more effective and rational decision making, allowing you to move away from compulsive behaviors.

There are various relaxed breathing methods that you can try; however, two seem to be the most common breathing patterns. The first one is the four in four out, and the second one is the 4, 7, 8 methods. For the four in four out method, you simply want to relax your body and begin breathing into the count of four and then breathing out to the count of four. This brings a rhythm to your breath and helps you to even it out; thereby, restoring calmness into your body. If you are experiencing a panic attack or are in any other extremely heightened state of energy, the four in four out method is great because it follows a consistent in-and-out rhythm.

The 4, 7, 8 method is slightly different as it requires a certain amount of holding your breath. For this method, you want to breathe into the count of four, hold your breath for the count of seven, and then breathe out for the count of eight. This is meant to gently bring your body back to a state of calmness by managing your stress through "overriding" your stress responses within your body. If you are feeling particularly panicked, holding your breath may not feel achievable so you may prefer to use the four in four out method, or start with the four in four out method and then progress to the 4, 7, 8 method as you begin to calm down. In doing so, you take back control over your automatic responses and train your body to begin experiencing peace even during uncomfortable or stressful experiences.

Part 3: Putting CBT to Work

Chapter 5: Behavioral Activation

Now that you have a strong understanding of the tools available to you in CBT, how they are used, when, and why, it is time for you to begin putting CBT into action in your own life! The very first step in CBT is engaging in a process known as behavioral activation. A behavioral activation is a form of therapeutic intervention that is used to integrate behavioral changes in an individual's day-to-day life. In this chapter, you are going to discover how you can use behavioral activation to begin making real adjustments in your lifestyle so that you can start overcoming your emotional symptoms and start experiencing more emotional freedom in your life.

How Does Behavioral Activation Work?

Behavioral activation is built on the belief that actions precede emotions. In other words, the way you spend your time impacts the mood that you are going to be in. Therefore, if you consistently spend your time behaving in unproductive ways, your mood will consistently remain troubling. Behavioral activation is most commonly used in treating things like depression or anxiety as it supports you in understanding and breaking your behavioral cycles so that you can begin experiencing a better life overall. However, this method can also be used in supporting you in successfully overcoming other troubling emotional symptoms too.

With behavioral activation, you have three primary goals. These are to identify the troubling cycle that is causing the distressing behaviors, to implement new behaviors, and to reward yourself for the new behaviors. These are believed to support you in breaking habits relating to your emotional struggles by halting the behaviors that are causing them while stimulating your mind to see these new behaviors as positive and enjoyable. By retraining your mind in this way, you condition yourself to begin acting in a way that supports you in feeling a greater sense of emotional wholeness and joy.

Conceptualizing Your Behavior Model

The first step in engaging in behavioral activation is recognizing what the behaviors are which prevent you from experiencing more positive emotions in your life. By identifying these cycles, you can pinpoint the exact behavior that is resulting in you not feeling better in your day-to-day life. This gives you the opportunity to change that behavior. The easiest way to identify what your exact cycle is will involve an activity log and consistent journaling in this log. You want to jot down nearly every activity that you are doing, what emotions coincide with that activity, and anything else that particularly stands out to you at that moment. By doing this over several days, you will begin to see patterns in your activities, just like you would in your thought records when you are tracking your thoughts.

After you have developed a log over several days to give you your starting point, you can begin to identify the exact cycle that you seem to go through. For example, you have been feeling depressed, and you feel as though you have no drive or motivation to begin doing anything in your life. If you were to look at your log, you might notice that you are feeling tired, and so, you decline invitations to go out and do things. Each time you decline an invitation, you feel bad which causes you to have even lower energy levels. This makes you less likely to go out and do anything in the near future, too. This leads to a constant cycle of lowered energies because you are no longer taking the time out of your day to do things that bring you joy and lift your spirits.

From the example above, you can see that the pinpointed problem was the fatigue or lowered energy levels causing you to avoid going out and doing anything in your free time. You need to pinpoint exactly where your problematic behaviors lie to give you a stronger understanding of what is causing you to experience your current emotional symptoms. Then, you can begin to develop a plan for how you are going to combat those problems to increase your positive feelings and decrease your negative or frustrating ones. In the above example, the problem was the low energy which led to you not engaging in the things that mattered to you anymore. The behavioral activation solution then would be to engage in more of what mattered, even if you were feeling a lowered sense of energy. By regularly engaging in the things that mattered to you, even if you had lowered energy and could only do so for a short period of time, you would be able to stop the spiral of feeling bad and further lowering your energy. Over time, the spiral will reverse, and you will begin feeling an increased sense of energy; thus, allowing you to essentially reverse your state of depression.

Behavioral Activation Techniques You Need to Know About

When it comes to conceptualizing your behavioral activation model and determining what course of action you are going to take to improve your emotional symptoms, you need to know what techniques are available for you to use. Those listed in Chapter 4 are incredibly supportive, but there are additional techniques that are specific to behavioral activation that you will likely need to use to experience success from this strategy.

The techniques that you need to know include:

• **Self-monitoring of activities and mood** (to see which behaviors are impacting your mood and whether or not your overall mood is improving)

• **Activity scheduling** (used to motivate you to do things particularly when you have been struggling to stay motivated, such as with depression)

• **Activity structuring** (used to adjust the structure of activities you are engaging in to support you in breaking the cycle of your difficult moods)

• **Problem-solving** (to support you in feeling strong enough in overcoming various struggles that you may face in your day-to-day life)

• **Social skill training** (to support you in feeling more confident in social situations so that you can overcome anxiety, depression, etc.)

• **Hierarchy construction** (the process of ranking activities based on how easy they are to accomplish, and then starting small and increasing your efforts as you go)

• **Shaping** (training yourself to begin engaging in healthier behaviors)

• **Reward** (stimulating your brain to see positive activities as rewarding and worthwhile in order to overcome thoughts like, *It does not matter,* or *I get no value from this*)

• **Persuasion** (persuading yourself to begin engaging in more positive behaviors so that you can overcome challenging emotional symptoms)

• **Behavior contract** (having your friends and family commit to only reinforcing healthy behaviors within you so that they are not enabling your troubling emotional experiences)

• **Life area assessment** (determining where it is that you actually want to experience success in your life and discovering what actually matters to you so that you can incorporate those things into your therapy)

Personalized Positive Activities

Once you have identified the problem areas in your behavioral cycles, you need to pick some personalized positive activities that you can swap these problematic behaviors out with. These activities will be used in alignment with the techniques mentioned above to support you in completely swapping out problematic behaviors and experiencing relief from troubling emotional symptoms. It is important that you choose activities that are relevant to you as attempting to engage in "positive" activities that do not matter to you may only result in you feeling worse by causing you to feel as though you are unable to feel better. In reality, the more likely cause is that you are attempting to feel better using positive activities that do not interest you or excite you; thus, rendering them useless for you.

A great way to begin identifying personalized positive activities is to simply sit down with a piece of paper and write down all of the things that make you feel good in your life. Write down which people you enjoy spending time with, what hobbies have brought you the most joy in the past, and what interests you have that cause you to feel active and engaged. Creating a list of things that make you feel good in your life will give you plenty of inspiration for things that you need to do when you recognize your negative behavioral cycle being activated so that you can swap out the negative behaviors for ones that make you feel better. For example, if you notice yourself about to say no to spending time with your friends because you are feeling a low sense of energy, you may instead agree to a quiet evening together or schedule for something in the near future. Then, instead of sitting around feeling bad about yourself, you can engage in something else that makes you feel positive so that you are engaging in activities that genuinely support you in feeling better.

Rewarding Yourself

The last thing you need to do when you are using behavioral activation is actually putting your concept into action by practicing your new positive activities. Every time you do, you need to reward yourself for doing so. This is how you are going to condition your mind to begin engaging in more positive behaviors and feeling as though the engagement is genuinely worth your while. Rewarding yourself will look different from person to person so you will need to determine what your best course of rewarding actions will be. You need to determine a series of rewards that will actually make you feel positive for engaging in your positive behaviors.

Again, the best way to know exactly what rewards are going to be a proper fit for you is to sit with your journal and determine what small things make you feel incredibly good in your life. This could be a favorite drink, small activity, or even a small object that makes you feel really good any time you receive it. Then, you simply grant yourself one of these rewards every time that you engage in positive activities that lead to you feeling better. This way, you feel more positive from the activity itself, and then you feel an even greater influx of positivity from the reward. Completing this new cycle will feel much like achieving a goal and receiving a tangible reward for it; thereby, causing an increase in dopamine in your brain and an easier ability to integrate the new cycle to go forward. As you continue integrating your positive behavioral cycle and experiencing all of the positive rewards associated with it, you will find that it becomes increasingly easier for you to build yourself up and adjust your behaviors through this repetitive practice.

Getting Back on the Horse

Any time you attempt to break old habits and replace them with new ones, you are going to experience difficulty in maintaining your new habits in the early stages. This is because your natural response to certain stimuli and triggers will be to engage in your previous habitual behaviors and not your new ones. It is important that you understand that these setbacks are not a negative reflection on you or your ability to feel better, but rather, they are a natural experience that everyone has. This is simply your brain trying to fulfill the cycle that feels natural, familiar, and comfortable to it. As you adjust your behavioral cycles to accommodate your new positive behaviors, the number of times that you engage in previous behaviors will decrease. Your brain will adapt to the positive experiences and begin understanding that there is a more effective method for getting its needs met that does not produce such a negative or uncomfortable result. When your brain begins to realize this, it will start adjusting to accommodate your new healthier habits and supporting you in the transitional process rather than resisting you.

Getting back on the horse requires you to truly understand that these backslides are in no way a reflection of you, your willpower, or your abilities. It is truly just a natural experience that everyone has. Simply get back on track when the next cycle is triggered and allow yourself to continue practicing until it becomes easier for you to engage in your positive behaviors on a consistent basis.

If you find that you are not thriving with your current action plan, you may benefit from reassessing your behavioral activation cycle and seeing if there is something that you may have missed. If you have continued to log your activities and moods since the beginning, which you should do, then you can also factor these into your consideration as you determine what may be holding you back from success. With this knowledge in mind, you can adjust your course of action so that you can begin experiencing greater success from your behavioral activation practices. You may need to continually reassess and adjust your plan a few times over before you find a system that truly works for you. Do not worry if it takes you some time, the more you focus on this process, the more likely you are to find success with using the behavioral activation strategy in your CBT.

Chapter 6: Change Your Core Beliefs

Our core beliefs are responsible for supporting us in interpreting the world around us and formulating opinions about the things that we see or experience in our lives. Our beliefs are typically formed in our childhoods; however, they can be shaped or introduced at any time with enough repetition or with a particularly strong emotional influence. For example, if a coworker bullied you on a constant basis and led you to believe that you are not good at your job, then you may begin to develop the belief that you are not capable. Or, if your coworker was to humiliate you in front of your boss or use a humiliating experience to validate why you are not good at your job, then you may associate this negative feeling with this negative opinion and thus formulate a negative belief that you are not capable.

Beliefs can be positive and helpful, or they can be negative and unproductive. The positive and helpful ones typically support us in living more positive lives by allowing us to see the best in life and to assess things in a way that supports us in feeling positively connected to the world around us. These beliefs do not need to be changed because they are helping you thrive in your life by allowing you to genuinely feel good and contribute positive things to the world around you.

Negative beliefs, however, are damaging and can result in you having unproductive and isolating experiences with the world around you. When you are experiencing negative beliefs, you may find yourself believing that you are not worthy or capable of being a part of society, that you have nothing to offer, or that you are a bad person. These types of beliefs can lead to you having an unhealthy mental atmosphere; thus, leading to negative thoughts that can produce negative emotions. All of which are the perfect foundation for emotional symptoms like anxiety or depression to thrive on. If you want to experience complete freedom from these troubling symptoms, you will need to learn how to change your negative beliefs so that they no longer limit your views on yourself and the world around you.

Changing your core beliefs requires you to identify what these beliefs are, pick the new beliefs that you want to switch them for, and then engage in the process of switching the beliefs around. When done correctly, you will completely mentally disconnect from the negative core belief that was limiting you so that you can attach to the more positive belief that expands your opportunities and opens your mind. In this chapter, we are going to explore what these very steps are and how you can begin practicing them in your own life.

Conceptualize the Swap

The first thing you need to do when it comes to switching your negative core belief for a positive one is to identify what exact beliefs you are trying to swap. You need to consider exactly what your negative core belief is and how it impacts you, then choose a positive core belief that you want to replace it with. You need to make sure that you completely understand the difference between your negative core belief and your positive core belief, including how both have impacted you in your life.

Identify why your negative core belief limited you and what types of troubles it has caused for you, including how it has contributed to your anxiety or depression. Then, identify what your new positive core belief will be like and how it will lift these limitations and support you in experiencing a more positive life going forward. For example, maybe your negative core belief was *I am not worthy,* and it led to you denying yourself the opportunity to try new things because you felt like you were not worthy of having a good time. If you were to replace this negative core belief with one like *I am worthy*, then the limitations of your unwillingness to try new things would be lifted because you would realize that you are worthy of enjoying yourself and trying new things. Get clear on what you are losing and what you are gaining. Realize that what you stand to gain is far more than what your negative core belief has ever given you.

Rate Your Beliefs

Once you know what beliefs you want to swap and the reason for it, you need to take a moment to honestly rate these beliefs regarding how much you genuinely believe in them. You will rate your beliefs on a scale of 0-100, where 0 means that you do not believe in said belief at all and 100 means that you believe in it completely. You need to rate both your negative core belief that you want to release and the positive core belief that you want to integrate into your life. You do not need the numbers to add up to 100 either. For example, you could say that you believe *I am unworthy* 80% and *I am worthy* 10%. If you are unsure as to what you want to rate these two beliefs, simply spend a few minutes considering each one and let yourself intuitively pick the number that feels right for you. You only need to be accurate towards what you are feeling. There is no index or system that you need to consider when you are rating these beliefs.

Identify the Nature of Your Negative Core Belief

It is important that you understand the nature of your negative core belief, or what type of negative core belief it is. There are two types of negative core beliefs that people tend to have: the stable ones and unstable ones. Stable negative core beliefs remain consistent no matter what, and virtually nothing that you experience in your life will change the fact that you have this negative core belief. Unstable negative core beliefs fluctuate with your mood, and this means that you may believe them more when you are sad as compared to when you are happy.

When you have a negative core belief that is stable, you believe it no matter how you feel and you likely cannot recall a time in the recent past where you did not believe it. This type of negative core belief can be slightly harder to change as it requires you to put more effort into finding evidence that it is not true or does not need to be true for you any longer. Unstable core beliefs can be easier to adjust because of the very fact that they fluctuate so much. It can be easier for you to assure yourself that they are untrue because you do not believe them nearly as much when you are feeling positive; thereby, helping you remind yourself that they are not true even when you are feeling negative.

Keep a Positive Forward Focus

Now that you have thoroughly addressed your situation, it is time to start putting a serious strategy toward the process of swapping out your negative core belief for a positive core belief. The method that you are going to use is simple, though it does require consistent practice. All you need to do to swap your beliefs are to consistently stay focused on your new positive core belief and strengthen your faith in it while ultimately ignoring the old negative core belief. The more you attempt to focus on dismantling your negative core belief, the less you are going to be able to do so because you will be regularly reinforcing it with attention and energy. The more you attempt to stop thinking about it or believing in it, the more your attention will focus on it. As you already know, our brains like to "check" to see if we are doing a good job at not doing something, which results in us mentally doing it anyway.

Adjusting your focus and keeping your attention on the positive core belief will allow you to invest your energy in the new belief that will actually support you in feeling better. Any time you find yourself considering your negative core belief, simply begin thinking about your preferred positive core belief instead. Do not attempt to dismantle, debunk, or demystify the negative core belief. Simply let it go and begin thinking about the new more positive belief instead. This will ensure that you are investing your time and energy into increasing your belief in the positive core belief; thus, allowing it to completely take the place of the old negative one.

Maintain a Data Log

Another great strategy for improving your ability to integrate your new positive core belief is to practice maintaining a data log. To do this, you need to commit to keeping a log about your new positive belief for at least two weeks. During these two weeks, you need to write down every single reason why your positive belief is true. This means that you need to consciously accumulate evidence that proves that it is true and write it down every single time you come across more evidence that supports your new belief. For example, say you want to boost your belief in the saying "I make money easily" and then you find a dollar on the ground. This would prove that you make money easily because a dollar came into your life with no efforts on your own.

By accumulating positive evidence that supports your positive core belief, you show your mind that this belief is, in fact, true and that it is safe for you to begin trusting in your new belief fully. Over time, your brain will realize that your evidence must be true and it will begin to increase the amount in which you believe in this new belief. Soon, your old negative core belief will no longer be relevant because there will be too much positive evidence supporting your new positive core belief.

Heal the Origins of the Old Belief

Sometimes, old negative core beliefs can be particularly hard to let go of because they are rooted in your childhood, and you have had them for a tremendously long time. As a child, your brain has not yet developed to the point that you are capable of realizing that you can have thoughts, beliefs, and opinions of your own. Instead, you still believe that you are deeply connected to your parents or guardians in your life, and you feel as though anything they think or believe must also be thought and believed by you. Often, these beliefs are developed not through a direct verbal transmission from your parents to you, but instead, through behaviors and the way that you perceive these behaviors. For example, if your parents never asked for your opinion about family matters, you may then believe that your opinion is invalid and therefore you believe that no one needs to listen to you or respect your opinion in life.

Taking the time to consider where your belief has come from, especially if it is rooted in your childhood, gives you the opportunity to actually heal the origins of your negative core belief so that it is easier for you to release it and replace it. This healing process may look different depending on how your belief came to be and what it felt like for you as you adopted the belief. However, it is important that you honor your body and mind as you go through the process of healing and allow for yourself to express whatever emotions that you may need to in order to heal. As long as you are not harming yourself or anyone else in the process, releasing your emotions is a great way to allow yourself to completely heal from the origins of negative core beliefs so that you can effectively replace them with new positive core beliefs.

Self-Monitor Your Behaviors

During the process of swapping out your beliefs, it is important that you self-monitor your behaviors. Many things may take place during the transitional process that can actually have a negative impact on your ability to swap out your beliefs. These include overcompensating for the negative core belief, surrendering to the belief, avoiding triggers, or feeling any emotional symptoms arising from the belief, such as anxiety or depression.

If you are overcompensating for your negative core belief, you will notice because it will feel as though you are trying far too hard to remove it. It may feel as though you are fighting yourself to integrate the positive core belief. This leads to you feeling overwhelmed, frustrated, and resentful towards yourself for not being able to integrate the new positive core belief. If you are experiencing this, you need to slow down and attempt a more moderate behavior to use alongside integrating your new core belief. For example, instead of aggressively and obsessively repeating your positive core belief in your mind, you could simply say it once and then choose to drop the topic of your beliefs altogether. You may also need to simply start acting as if you believe the new belief even if you do not necessarily believe it just yet. It can take a few months for this to fully work, so be patient with yourself and do not grow frustrated, aggressive or obsessive if it does not start working right away. Remember, your negative beliefs have likely had a long time to root themselves into your mind and have a negative impact on your life. If you want to release them, you will need to be patient and give your new positive core beliefs just as much time to integrate themselves and take root in your mind, too.

If you are surrendering to the negative core belief, you need to stop and consider why you believe in it. Any time you notice yourself surrendering to the negative core belief by modifying your behavior or thoughts to accommodate for it, you need to confront this behavior and then begin acting as if you believe your new positive core belief. If you allow yourself to continually surrender to the negative core belief, you will find that it is impossible for you to change because you are avoiding the opportunity to change your belief out for a new positive one. The same is true for any instance where you find yourself avoiding triggers because you do not want to be confronted by your negative core belief. If you do not expose yourself to the situations that grant you the opportunity to make changes, you are not going to have access to what you need to genuinely facilitate changes in your life.

If you find that your mood is low and you have not been consciously aware of your thoughts or beliefs for some time, take a minute to reflect on your negative core belief and see what may be going on with it. You may discover that you have been unconsciously buying into the belief and allowing yourself to be shaken by it. Any time you find yourself feeling anxious or depressed, honestly ask yourself how much you are buying into the negative core belief on a scale of 0-100. If you realize that you have been buying into it quite a bit, give yourself the opportunity to release from it by consciously using this as a chance to integrate your new positive core belief instead.

Chapter 7: Mindfulness-integrated CBT

Mindfulness-integrated CBT or MiCBT is a CBT approach that incorporates the power of mindfulness with a standard of CBT practices. Using MiCBT, trained therapists have been able to address a variety of psychological disorders in their clients and support them in experiencing full healing from these disorders. Mindfulness and CBT fit together perfectly as they both involve a self-healing approach when it comes to addressing emotional symptoms of psychological disorders and correcting the behaviors and thought processes that may be contributing to them.

Mindfulness, or mind-fullness, means to approach life with your mind fully attentive to the world around you. Your objective when engaging in mindfulness is to bring your awareness completely into the present moment and engage in it with a non-judgmental, nonreactive, and accepting attitude. Mindfulness allows you to begin experiencing life alongside a healthy form of detachment that allows you to gain the most out of every moment without feeling so personally open and vulnerable to the world around you. As a result, addressing things like stress, anxiety, and depression becomes easier because you are not using the world around you to reinforce your inner beliefs that promote the development of stress, anxiety, and depression.

When combined with CBT, mindfulness amplifies your capacity to adjust your behaviors so that you can lessen the impact of your psychological disorders and experience emotional freedom from them. MiCBT integrates both mindfulness and CBT into a therapeutic process that takes place over four stages. This chapter will explain these four stages to you, including how to engage in them.

The Four Stages

The four-stage process of MiCBT allows individuals to improve the way they are feeling and progressively change their unhelpful behaviors. Unlike CBT, which works predominantly on thoughts and beliefs that lead to unwanted behaviors, MiCBT seeks to help you develop control over the processes that are allowing you to maintain these unrealistic thoughts and beliefs. Thus, your focus is not only to change the content of your thoughts but to change the entire process that leads up to the content, too.

The four stages that you will encounter in MiCBT include the personal stage, the exposure stage, the interpersonal stage, and the empathetic stage. Each of these stages is designed to support you in progressively getting to the root cause of each thought process and neutralize the impact that they have on you. At each stage, you will engage in different practices and techniques to support you in fully grasping the purpose of the stage and the lessons within it before moving on to the next stage.

Personal Stage

The personal stage is stage 1 in MiCBT. This stage is devoted to teaching you about mindfulness skills so that you can begin to discover how you can let go of unhelpful thoughts and emotions so that you can successfully address life's challenges. Your goal in stage 1 is to develop equanimity so that you can begin experiencing life from a more neutral perspective. This is how you can stop feeling as though you are personally being victimized by other people's thoughts, actions, and behaviors, as well as your own. Here, you learn how to stop taking everything quite so personally so that you can start assessing things with greater reason rather than being hijacked by your emotions.

To successfully begin practicing the personal stage, you need to start learning how to tune into your own thoughts and pay closer attention to them. A great way to do this is through mindfulness meditations where you sit and allow yourself to enter a meditative state before allowing yourself to become aware of what your thoughts are and how they are impacting you. You can also practice what is known as a "body scan" whereby you direct your conscious awareness to various areas of your body so that you can become aware of any sensations or tension that may be present in that area of your body. These types of practices allow you to become aware of your own inner voice that continues to chat with you in your mind even if you are not always consciously aware of it.

As you continue growing more consciously aware of your intuition and your inner voice, you can begin using this to support you in mindfully detaching from the world around you. This mindful-detachment, or equanimity, is not intended to isolate you but is instead used as a way to neutralize your perspective of the world around you. Mindfulness will support you in doing this by allowing you to become aware of your inner voice and what it may be saying to you and detach from it any time you recognize that the voice is seeking to stir an unnecessary emotional response from you. For example, if you are in a public space and you begin experiencing anxiety because your inner voice tells you something bad is going to happen and you have no reason to believe that such is true, you can override it with evidence disproving your inner voice. From there, you can prevent or slow down the unwanted emotional response and begin addressing the environment around you with a rational response instead.

Exposure Stage

In stage 2, or the exposure stage, your goal is to begin learning how to self-regulate yourself in situations that you may have been avoiding in the past. So, in stage 1, your focus would have been learning how to build up your skills during your regular day-to-day life without pushing yourself to engage in any overly triggering experiences.

In stage 2, you want to intentionally begin exposing yourself to the things that trigger your psychological responses, such as anxiety or depression, so that you can begin to build confidence in yourself and in your abilities. The more you expose yourself to these triggering situations and successfully engage in self-regulation, the more confident you are going to feel in yourself and in the control that you have over your responses to the world around you. This is going to allow you to feel more confident in addressing challenging situations so that you can genuinely believe in your capacity to control your thoughts and emotions at any given time.

As you move into the exposure stage, it is important that you do not do so before you are ready to. Remember, your goal here is to build up your confidence, so you do not want to risk that by overexposing yourself and reinforcing your theory that these more challenging situations are dangerous and that you are incapable of handling them. Ideally, you should begin by exposing yourself to things that you would consider to be smaller triggers first. For example, they make you feel anxious but not so anxious that you could not possibly handle them even if your anxiety was triggered. Gradually increasing the severity of the trigger as you go along will support you in feeling a greater sense of confidence in yourself and your self-regulation skills. This will ensure that you are ready to handle the larger and more daunting tasks as they come along; thereby, allowing you to experience full success from your MiCBT.

If you do find yourself overexposed and feeling a lack of confidence in any given situation, it is important that you take the time to mindfully draw your awareness to reality and recognize that you are in the process of healing and that, sometimes, setbacks are going to happen. Giving yourself the opportunity to rationally consider what happened and mindfully become aware of how you can improve in the future, while also disengaging from the emotions relating to your setback, will support you in feeling more confident going forward.

Interpersonal Stage

As you move into stage 3, or the interpersonal stage, you are going to begin developing a stronger interpersonal understanding, as well as improving your communication skills in challenging situations. Here, you will gain the opportunity to learn how to respond to other people's reactivity, rather than react back and escalate the situation; thus, deteriorating the quality of the interaction and increasing the chance of a negative experience.

In this stage, you want to use your mindfulness to help you identify your thoughts and feelings and recognize how they are impacting you in your day-to-day life. Then, as you go about your daily life and begin to feel the arousal of thoughts and feelings that could indicate the oncoming of an anxious or depressive episode, you need to begin enforcing new strategies instead. You will start by mentally slowing down the process and taking a moment to assess what your thoughts and emotions are, and what your goal is in the present situation. For example, your boss wants to talk to you, and this elicits an anxious response within you. Rather than attempting to avoid the conversation or bringing a severe amount of anxiety into the conversation with you, you could instead recognize your anxiety and your anxious thoughts and consider what their goal is. Maybe you are worried about getting in trouble, so your goal is to avoid having an uncomfortable conversation about your poor work ethic of late. Your goal, then, would be to have a constructive conversation that does not cause hurt feelings or a sense of deep shame in you. You could start by recalling equanimity and intentionally practicing healthy detachment from the situation so that you could then address it from a neutral perspective. Through this, you may realize that there are many possible reasons for why your boss would want to talk to you, and not only to reprimand you for the work that you have been doing.

Once you have slowed down your thoughts and emotions and given yourself a chance to rationally process what your goal is, you can choose a more rational response to the conversation that you are about to encounter. For example, if you do go in to have the conversation with your boss and it turns out that they do want to talk to you about your recent work ethic, instead of allowing yourself to react with anxiety, you can slow down and choose to respond with calmness. Rather than growing so anxious that you can hardly focus, you can instead listen to what your boss has to say, respond thoughtfully, and agree to implement any changes into your routine to improve your work ethic. This way, you can have a productive conversation with your boss without finding yourself being sucked away into your anxious response and struggling to remain professional and attentive during the conversation.

If you find yourself entering a conversation with someone who is experiencing a high level of reactivity to the situation, such as by getting excessively angry or anxious, this stage will also support you in learning how to detach from the other person's reactivity. In doing so, you will be able to guide yourself through the process of having a more thoughtful and intentional response. This helps you avoid stumbling into your own unwanted emotional symptoms. This can also help you refrain from having reactive conversations that become escalated by both you and the other individual; thereby, potentially leading to an unwanted situation, such as an intense argument or a challenging panic attack.

Empathetic Stage

The fourth and final stage of the MiCBT process is the empathetic stage. During the empathetic stage, you will discover how you can experience an increased sense of empathy and compassion towards yourself and others in daily interactions. This will increase your sense of self-worth while also supporting you in developing a deep sense of care and connection with those around you. This helps you to develop stronger relationships with both yourself and others. This allows you to experience the fulfillment of one thing that every human needs, which is a genuine connection with others.

During the empathetic stage, you want to teach yourself to see others as human beings who have human responses to the world around them. Here, you can take the time to recognize that not everyone is actively aware of how their behavior impacts themselves and others and they may not be ready to deal with this information yet. In fact, some people may never be ready to take responsibility for their actions and how their behaviors and beliefs impact both themselves and everyone around them. In learning to experience empathy for these people, you discover how to stop blaming everyone around you for the negative way that they may impact your life. Instead, you allow yourself to see them for who they are. If you need to, you can detach from them and terminate your relationship with the said person to preserve your own sense of wellbeing. The goal here is to stop holding such deep resentments towards others for their actions so that you can stop taking their actions personally.

You also need to learn how to increase the amount of empathy and compassion that you feel for yourself so that you can stop blaming and resenting yourself every time you make a mistake in your life. In realizing that you, too, are only human and that you are also susceptible to making mistakes and growing at your own pace, you let yourself off the hook for things that you have done in your life.

This allows you to begin forgiving yourself and releasing the shame that you may carry from the way that you have acted or behaved in your past. It can also support you in feeling more forgiving towards yourself during the growing process as you learn how to do things in a better way and become the best version of you. Instead of holding yourself to impossibly high standards and then feeling anxious or depressed when you cannot meet them, you can hold yourself to reasonable, human-level standards, and feel proud of yourself when you try your best.

Developing this type of empathy in stage four ultimately requires you to continue practicing self-regulation and honestly assessing your thoughts and emotions from moment to moment. By mindfully addressing them and restoring your rational thinking processes, you can bring your emotions back into balance and prevent yourself from experiencing such an intense spiral of negative or unwanted emotional responses. Here, you allow yourself to fully have control over your mind and emotions and experience the world around you free of your troubling emotional symptoms.

Part 4: Supportive CBT Practices

Chapter 8: Increasing Mental Stamina

In CBT, the best way to achieve your goals is to have practices that are both focused on overcoming unwanted behavioral challenges while also improving your life in general. The practices that are specifically focused on supporting you in overcoming unwanted behavioral challenges, such as behavioral activation or MiCBT, are going to be the tools that help you overcome specific challenges. Supportive CBT practices will allow you to reinforce your life with positive behaviors so that you can improve your life in general. This makes you more resilient to the development of future problematic behaviors. In other words, by practicing supportive CBT practices, you improve your chances of experiencing full relief from challenging psychological disorders, such as anxiety and depression, by strengthening your mind and wellness overall.

This chapter introduces you to support practices that can increase your mental stamina and help you feel a stronger sense of general wellness and control within your mind. This will be supportive in helping you feel as though you and your mind are on the same page and that you can truly work together with yourself to overcome any challenges that you may have regarding your thoughts and emotions. This also helps you with developing a strong relationship with yourself so that you can feel a greater general sense of positivity concerning your own being.

Improving Your Problem-Solving Abilities

Not having a strong ability to solve problems in your life can lead you to feel overwhelmed in the face of uncertainty. People who struggle with their problem-solving abilities often find themselves feeling a lack of confidence around trying new things or engaging in uncertain experiences because they fear that if something goes wrong, they will not know what to do. This type of uncertainty can spark a fear of being endangered without the necessary skills to survive, even though most situations are not actually life-threatening. From this state, the development of anxiety is only natural. As your anxiety begins to develop, you find yourself unwilling to try new things out of fear of being vulnerable without the necessary skills to protect yourself. If you consistently decline new things because of this fear, it can also leave you feeling depressed, which can further deteriorate the quality of your mental health.

Learning how to improve your problem-solving abilities means that you equip yourself with the skills required to navigate uncertain situations so that you no longer experience such a deep sense of vulnerability in these experiences. Essentially, you build your trust in yourself and in your capacity to survive no matter what experiences you may face. One great way to improve your problem-solving skills is by playing logic-based puzzles or games. Things like Sudoku or riddles are designed to encourage you to start thinking critically so that you can discover what the solution is to the puzzle or the problem. Regularly engaging in these problem-solving games is a great way to increase your capacity to solve problems. This allows you to feel more confident in your problem-solving abilities. Mindfulness is also a great practice when it comes to problem-solving as it teaches you how you can detach from intense emotional responses so that you can assess situations from a rational state of mind. Bringing yourself back into rational thinking improves your decision-making skills as well as your problem-solving skills, which will then allow you to address challenges in your life with a clearer perspective.

Using Mantras and Meditation

Mantras and meditation are a great way to improve your mental state by helping you improve your mindfulness while also allowing you to feel a greater sense of freedom from intrusive or negative thoughts. Mantras, or personal mottos, are a great way to empower yourself and inspire yourself to see things from a more resilient, confident, and positive perspective. Your personal mantra can be anything that you desire it to be, so long as it supports you in feeling empowered and inspired to overcome any challenges that you may face in your life. You can also change your personal mantra or use a couple if you feel that you need empowerment in multiple areas of your life.

Your mantra can be repeated at any time that you need extra mental support in overcoming adversity in your life. It can also be repeated during meditation as a way to reinforce your mantra in your mind so that it is even stronger when you use it actively in your day-to-day life. Mantra-based meditations can involve you meditating and then chanting your mantra over and over to yourself, or you can simply say it to yourself quietly in your mind and allow yourself to feel overcome by the power of your mantra.

Meditating itself is also highly valuable. While meditating alongside mantras can be extremely powerful, using meditation on its own can improve your mindfulness as well as support you in feeling a deeper sense of relaxation in your life. From a mindfulness front, meditating gives you the opportunity to become more aware of what types of thoughts are residing in your mind and how they may be making you feel. The goal is to recognize the thoughts and the accompanying feelings without attempting to judge them or manipulate them in any way. Instead, you simply want to become aware of them so that you can gain an honest understanding as to what is going on inside of you at that moment. From a relaxation perspective, meditation allows you to sit with yourself and experience peace from the world around you; thus, giving you the opportunity to "offload" anything that may be causing you to feel overwhelmed or stressed out. The more you meditate, the less residual stress you carry with you; thus, making future stressful situations less overwhelming for you to endure.

Soaking in the Healing Benefits of Nature

Nature has an incredibly healing impact on humans. Even though we have boxed ourselves up in homes, surrounded ourselves in cement, and confined a significant amount of nature to either garden beds or allocated forests, we still crave nature in the very center of our beings. Getting out and being one with nature for any period of time can have a significantly healing impact on your life. Nature allows you to remove yourself from the hustle and grind of day-to-day living and immerse yourself in an entire ecosystem where the motto seems to be "let it be" as everything just does what it pleases at any given moment. Plenty can be learned through nature and plenty of healing that can be done in its presence.

Forest bathing and tree-hugging are considered to be two incredibly powerful practices to support you in overcoming mental distress and feeling a sense of peace in your life. Forest bathing, or simply spending time in a forest, allows you to relax in a quiet and serene place and simply watch the world exist around you. In the forest, there is no agenda, sense of time, or pressing need to get anything done. Instead, the forest is completely devoted to being in the moment and living peacefully amongst those around you. If you hug a tree while you are there, you can use this as an opportunity to slow down and truly physically connect yourself to one of the most serene life forms in the entire forest. Trees have plenty to offer when it comes to learning about mindfulness as they spend their entire lives focused solely on growing up toward the sunlight and standing strong in their place. Trees do not walk, run, or crawl. They are stationary and spend their entire long lives building themselves up in just one spot. Soaking in the slow and focused energy of the tree for a moment can support you in remembering that not everything has to be fast and that some of the biggest things in life come from the slowest and smallest efforts.

Another way that you can engage with nature is through bird watching. Bird watching is incredibly peaceful, but it also gives you the opportunity to be mindful. When you are watching birds, you must sit still and remain quiet so that you do not scare the birds away. Your patience and calmness is required, which encourages you to learn how you can sit quietly and enjoy the peace around you as the birds that you are watching live their lives. Plus, the very act of watching carefree animals enjoy their lives without any stress or concerns is a wonderful way to remember the true values of life and to restore peace into your own mind.

Finally, if you want to get out into nature and physically engage with it, gardening is a great hobby that is both peaceful and productive. The act of gardening itself allows you to remove yourself from your typical environment and focus your energy on something that is relaxing and slower. You can focus your time on tilling soil, planting seeds, watering your garden, pulling weeds, or simply checking in on things to make sure that everything is growing healthily. As you are in your garden, you can commit to spending this time by only paying attention to your garden and what is happening within your garden. Plus, with a garden, you are remaining productive by teaching yourself to stay focused and achieve long-term goals successfully. Gardens take time, patience, and consistency which are three mental practices that can change your mental world completely when it comes to learning how to overcome anxiety, depression, and other psychological disorders. As you continue gardening, you will begin to reap in the rewards of your practices with the healthy plants that grow under your care, which allows you to feel accomplished and meaningful.

Finding Value in Feeling Small

One of the biggest reasons why people experience anxiety or depression is because they feel insignificant. Feeling insignificant can be exhausting, upsetting, and painful. Often, feeling insignificant can leave you feeling unworthy and like there is nothing for you to live for because you are not significant enough to have value. Of course, this is not true, though, the feelings of insignificance can lead you to believe that is the case.

If you want to stop feeling the pain associated with feeling insignificant, you can start finding the value in feeling small. Feeling small could make you feel insignificant, *or* it could be seen as an opportunity to relieve yourself from the weight of the world that you have been carrying on your shoulders.

If you find yourself feeling personally responsible for solving all of the world's problems and helping everyone in your life to feel better or experience better things, feeling small can lead you to believe that you are incapable of fulfilling your purpose. This is painful for anyone to experience. However, if you put life back into perspective and realize that it is not your job to personally solve all of the world's problems and make everyone feel better, suddenly, being small is not such a bad thing.

Being small means that you are not required to oversee everything and cure every problem that the world faces. You can now confidently focus on yourself and your needs. This is because *it is not your responsibility to fulfill the needs of anyone else but yourself.* Since it is not your responsibility to manage anyone else's emotions or needs but yourself, you can feel good about focusing all of your energy and attention on fulfilling your needs and helping yourself feel better. Then, from this state of feeling better, you can even support others in having a better life themselves – if you desire to. The key difference here is that you are doing it from a state of personal power and feeling in control of yourself and your feelings, rather than feeling as though it is your obligation to fulfill everyone else's needs and never feeling as though you have the energy to do so.

If feeling small gives you a feeling of fear, like you are too small to matter to anyone else, you will need to spend some time genuinely assessing the reality behind this. Is it true that you do not matter, or is this an overgeneralization that you are telling yourself? If you are being honest with yourself, you will know that this is an overgeneralization and that it is not true because you do matter and to many other people in the world, too, whether you realize it or not. The best way to combat this situation is to develop evidence that proves that you matter no matter how big or small you may feel.

Stargazing and Cloud Watching

Similar to getting out into nature or watching birds fly about their day, stargazing and cloud watching are two powerful ways to increase your relaxation and plug yourself into a mindfulness practice. For some people, complete meditation practices simply do not feel achievable, especially if you have been living with a significant amount of stress in your life on a day-to-day basis for quite some time. Releasing the need to do meditation, look for any specific way and engage in meditative practices. Stargazing or cloud watching is a great way to gain the same benefits without feeling the pressure to sit still and bring yourself into a relaxed state.

One great thing about stargazing and cloud watching is that they are fairly accessible activities for virtually anyone to enjoy. Even if you struggle with mobility issues, are feeling a particularly low sense of motivation, or it is too cold to go outside, you can still engage in these activities. Simply sit next to your window and look out into the sky and see what arises in front of you. As you do, allow yourself to be whisked away in the daydreams that arise and allow yourself to engage in all the same practices that you would during traditional meditation. Notice the thoughts and emotions, do not judge them or attempt to shape them and accept them for what they are. This way, you can gain all of the values of meditating without actually having to go out and meditate.

Healing Through Art and Music

Art and music are two great ways to process what is on your mind and express yourself in an incredibly powerful way. What's the best part? You do not have to be an incredible artist or a musician to let these two art forms support you in healing. Art and music are both used in many different forms of therapy as a way to help people express themselves when they feel as though they cannot put what they feel into words. Engaging in the arts as a way of strengthening your mind can involve admiring other people's artwork or music, or creating your own. There is no right or wrong way to go about this. Simply getting you involved is powerful enough.

If you choose to create artwork, you can do so in any different number of ways. Simpler art forms like macaroni frames and tapping a tambourine can be incredibly therapeutic and offers just as much expressional release as more complex art forms like painting landscapes or composing a new song. Engaging in just a few minutes of artwork per day or a few hours per week can support you in feeling a stronger sense of release from the emotions and thoughts that you are experiencing inside. One great thing about art is that even though it is a gentle expression, it is still a physical expression. The process of moving your hands through the motion of creating can support you in physically moving the energy of your thoughts and emotions out of your body so that you can begin to experience energetic and emotional release from them.

If you find that creating art on your own is not helpful or that you want to create something more complex than what you already know how to do, joining an art class is a great way to expand your skills while also committing to art on a regular basis. Painting classes, guitar lessons, drawing classes, or even simply coloring with a group of friends can be a great way to engage in art on a regular basis and gain the therapeutic values of this activity.

If creating art is not of interest to you, you might consider admiring it. Listening to music or attending art galleries is a great way to connect with other people through the unspoken method of artistry. Sometimes, seeing something on paper or hearing a specific sound through a song will resonate with you and the feelings or thoughts that you are having. These types of connections help you feel as though another human being understands you. They also help you begin to discover a new way for you to express yourself when you lack the words to formulate the correct expression on your own. In many cases, admiring other people's artwork is a powerful way to expose your own thoughts and emotions to yourself so that you can make better sense of them, and then you can find your own method of expression after the fact.

The Power of Writing

Like art and music, writing is a powerful way to strengthen your mind and keep yourself feeling mentally whole and complete. Writing can be done in almost any way that you please, as long as you are actively engaging in it on a regular basis. Poetry and creative writing are two great ways to release what is on your mind through creative expression in the form of words. Through these two forms of writing, you do not necessarily have to dig into literal representations of what you are feeling or write specifically about your thoughts and feelings. Instead, you can translate your thoughts and feelings into a work of art that expresses yourself but allows you to keep the personal details out of it.

Alternatively, you might consider picking up a different type of writing, such as journaling. Journaling on a regular basis can support you in releasing the things that are on your mind in a more factual and complete manner. Through journaling, you can say exactly what you think and feel without any fear of another person reading it or trying to make sense of it. In your journal, you can write what you feel that you cannot say out loud to other people. Because of this ability, to be honest, you can support yourself in expressing what you are feeling and process it more completely so that you do not feel as though you are stuck holding onto it inside. This can help release feelings of shame and guilt, amongst other painful emotions, and allows you to completely heal from anything that may be bothering you or keeping you feeling trapped in emotional distress.

Chapter 9: Increase Physical Wellness

In addition to keeping your mind healthy, you also need to keep your body healthy. In CBT, your physical actions are believed to impact your thoughts and emotions directly. By keeping your physical actions focused on maintaining your overall health and supporting your wellness, you can tell your mind that you matter and that you deserve to be taken care of. With psychological disorders like depression, not taking care of your physical self is a common symptom that can further deteriorate the way you feel and your ability to bounce back from depressive episodes. Taking care of yourself can help you combat these feelings and behave in a way that keeps your depression at bay by ensuring that you feel good overall. Furthermore, you ensure that your body's physical systems are functioning healthily which supports the healthy functioning of your brain; therefore, promoting a more positive mindset overall.

When it comes to increasing your physical wellness with the specific aim of supporting your CBT efforts, there are four main areas that you want to pay attention to. These are food and water, hygiene, physical activity, and resting. By paying attention to these four areas and behaving in a way that promotes their health, you ensure that you stay physically healthy; thus, promoting your healthier mindset.

Eating a Healthy Diet

When you are experiencing things such as anxiety and depression, staying on top of your dietary habits is not always easy. With both conditions, it is not uncommon to avoid eating often because you genuinely feel as though you are not hungry. The reality is that you are hungry; however, your increased stress has resulted in your appetite being suppressed so that the energy that would be used to digest food can instead be used to manage your symptoms of stress. Because of this suppressed appetite, it is not uncommon to completely avoid eating or to find yourself only eating the things you absolutely crave. Eating this way for a prolonged period of time can result in your body becoming even more stressed because it lacks the nutrients that it needs to thrive. Once your body begins to lack vital nutrients, a whole slew of other issues can arise. This can lead to increased stress, increased anxiety and depression, decreased resiliency, decreased immune system functions, and many other troubling symptoms that can further impede your ability to experience a healthy life, including emotionally.

Focusing on eating a good healthy diet on a day-to-day basis is important if you want to nourish your body and reduce the number of stress hormones being produced inside of you. If you need to, start with eating small healthy meals or snacks throughout the day as a way to begin building up your appetite. As your body grows used to these smaller meals and snacks, you will be able to continually increase the amount of food that you are eating on a consistent basis until you find yourself consuming healthy portions daily.

In some cases, your diet can be used to help combat emotional disturbances, too. For example, if you are experiencing depression, increasing the number of B vitamins and omega fatty acids that you consume has been said to be very supportive in managing your moods. If you are experiencing anxiety, decreasing your caffeine intake and eliminating other stimulating substances from your diet can support you in gaining more control over your anxiety.

Drinking Plenty of Water

Like food, many people who are experiencing anxiety or depression will also forget to drink a healthy amount of water on a day-to-day basis. Dehydration is another factor that can increase the number of stress hormones being produced within your body. It can produce troubling symptoms that can worsen your mood, such as headaches. Increasing your water intake and ensuring that you are consuming three liters of water every single day can support you in staying healthy and keeping your body happy. Water is essential in supporting your brain which is made up of 73% water so that it can function healthily.

If you struggle to drink enough water on a daily basis, try setting a reminder in your phone and carry a water bottle with you everywhere you go. Any time you experience even a small amount of thirst, take a sip of water. Begin training yourself to drink when you are thirsty so that you can ensure that you remain well-hydrated and that your body does not suffer increased stress due to dehydration.

Maintaining Your Personal Hygiene

Personal hygiene is another part of our daily routine that tends to be overlooked when we are experiencing intense anxiety or depression. Simple activities like brushing your teeth or hair or taking a shower may seem pointless when you are experiencing depression. You may find yourself feeling as though you lack the energy to stand up long enough to get the job done, so you simply avoid it altogether. Avoiding personal hygiene is not only unhealthy for you, but it also worsens your mood and leads to you having an increased likelihood of remaining depressed or anxious.

For example, if you are too depressed to shower, you avoid going out because you feel as though your hair looks greasy and you smell somewhat like body odor. Because of this, you might decline going out with friends because you are embarrassed about the way you look. You declining offers to go out not only prevents you from engaging in experiences that could boost your mood but also keeps you feeling bad about yourself because the primary reason you declined was that you were feeling embarrassed about yourself. This can seriously lower self-esteem and self-confidence and makes it even harder for you to break your mood and feel free from your depression.

Even if you don't feel like it, make an honest effort to at least shower, brush your hair, and brush your teeth on a day-to-day basis. Keeping up your basic hygiene practices will improve your health and keep you feeling a small sense of pride and confidence in yourself even if you are feeling particularly low.

Caring About Your Looks

Your looks do not dictate your worth, but they can have a massive impact on your mood overall. If you consistently look like you do not care about yourself, such as by not brushing your hair and wearing dirty clothes that don't fit or that don't go well together, you are going to feel like you do not care about yourself either. When people see you, whether you realize it or not, you are going to feel a sense of embarrassment because you have not taken pride in the way you look.

Caring about your looks does not mean that you have to be vain or that you have to apply makeup or put hours of effort into your appearance. Instead, it simply means that you take the time to clean yourself up and dress up nicely so that you look as though you care about yourself. When you behave as you care, your mind begins to recognize this and produces the feelings of caring too. You also begin to feel better because you can take pride in your looks when you go out in public. You do not feel as though you have to avoid the public, look away in shame, or feel embarrassed for how you look. Instead, you can feel proud about yourself and your appearances.

Getting Regular Activity

Physical activity is not only great for supporting a healthy body, but it is also great for supporting a healthy mind. When you participate in a regular activity, you allow yourself to release any built-up energy that may be lingering in your body and producing feelings of depression or anxiety. Ideally, you should engage in at least 30 minutes of intentional physical activity on a daily basis or about 200 minutes per week. If you are struggling to incorporate physical activity into your routine, you can break these minutes up into short bursts so that it does not feel like such a big amount of pressure. For example, if you are feeling extremely depressed and the idea of 30 minutes of walking or yoga feels overwhelming, you can simply dedicate five minutes to stretching. Then, an hour or two later, you can do another five minutes of stretching. Do this every hour or two until you have fulfilled your thirty minutes per day. As you begin to feel better from getting up and moving, you can start elongating your workouts until you are successfully getting a healthy amount of physical movement for 30 minutes per day.

If you struggle with physical activity due to mobility issues, consider talking to your doctor and discovering what types of activity you can safely do. Even simple things like stretching, yoga, swimming, or just getting outside to work in the garden can support you in getting some physical movement into your daily routine so that you can start feeling better about yourself and in your life.

Relaxing on Purpose

Many people fail to make time for relaxing on purpose and mistake it for sitting on the couch with their feet up as they scroll social media and read about stressful topics or listen to other people flock their negativity around. True and complete relaxation allows you to release stress from your mind and engage in peaceful activities. This can be watching a funny show on TV, reading, taking a bath or a relaxing shower, cooking or baking, or even just laying back on the couch with your eyes closed daydreaming about life.

Relaxing on purpose gives you time to unplug and tune out from the world around you. During this time, you want to release yourself from the pressure of the world and give yourself the freedom to just "be" with no strings attached. If you have a big family or find yourself living in a home that is not relaxing for you, you might consider engaging in some other form of relaxing activity on a regular basis. Going to a spa, sitting at the park, attempting float therapy, or engaging in other solo activities can be extremely helpful. You don't have to be alone if you would prefer to relax in the presence of someone else. Even having a quiet evening on the couch with your family as you watch a funny movie can be relaxing. The goal is to engage in any activity that is going to allow you to release yourself from the stressful demands of life and simply enjoy yourself.

Getting Proper Sleep

Rest is powerful, and unfortunately, many people do not get proper sleep every single night. When you are depressed or anxious, you might find yourself feeling extremely tired on a regular basis. In fact, you might even find yourself sleeping more often than not, potentially causing you to wonder why you are still so tired despite getting plenty of rest. The reality is that when you are depressed or anxious, your mind is often too stressed out to allow you to experience a true and deep rest. Instead, your sleep is typically light and restless or filled with nightmares that result in you feeling stressed out and uncomfortable in your sleep.

Getting a healthy sleep every single night is important, and it can be accomplished even if you do not feel as though you are getting enough rest right now. It does take some intention and practice, however, especially if you have been having particularly restless sleep each night. Using nightmare rescripting can be a great way to relax the state of your sleep even if you are not necessarily experiencing nightmares. This CBT practice can support you in restructuring your sleep state in general so that you can experience greater relief from any stress that may be following you into your sleep each night.

You can also improve the state of your sleep by meditating before bed using aromatherapy, keeping your bedroom clean and tranquil, ensuring that your bedding is comfortable, and by keeping your house at the right temperature. Avoiding stimulants in the evenings and night times and switching to relaxing foods and teas like those infused with chamomile and lavender is a great way to relax your body from the inside out. You also need to make sure that you are sleeping on a consistent schedule. Even though you may feel exhausted every single day, maintaining a consistent bedtime and wake time and avoiding sleeping in between can ensure that your body becomes used to sleeping on a consistent schedule. This can help you overcome feelings of chronic exhaustion and support you in feeling better rested when you wake up. Be kind to yourself if it takes a while to level out your sleep. These patterns do take time and are not something that will change right away. Several weeks on a consistent sleeping schedule with a strong and consistent bedtime routine can be extremely helpful though.

Chapter 10: Maintaining Wellness

Putting in the effort to heal yourself from troubling emotions like depression and anxiety only matters if you are going to continue putting in the effort to maintain your wellness. If you immediately stop practicing your wellness approach the moment you start experiencing relief from your symptoms, or if you throw in the towel when you do not see the results you desire, you can guarantee that your results will not come. You need to stay devoted and continue supporting your healing practices even long after you feel relief from the symptoms that were disturbing you for so long. By maintaining your wellness on an ongoing basis, you can ensure that you experience complete ongoing relief from your psychological disorders so that they do not slowly creep back in after you have spent so much time healing from them.

The following practices are things you can do to maintain your mental wellness on an ongoing basis.

Regularly Assessing Your Approach

As you continue down the path of healing yourself from depression and anxiety, it is imperative that you regularly assess your approach and make sure that you are having the best impact on your overall health that you possibly can. Reassessing your approach on a consistent basis allows you to ensure that you are always using the best approach possible and that you are making significant improvements on a regular basis. If you find that your approach is not effective or that it is not giving you the results you desire, you can take a moment to consider what about your approach may be holding you back. Then, you can accommodate for the necessary adjustments.

Reassessing your approach also gives you the opportunity to determine when you can successfully move to the next stage of your healing. For example, if you have been using your approach consistently for several months and you are experiencing success with it, you might find that you no longer need to use the same intensive approach because you have made so much progress. Instead, you can transition to a more moderate approach that allows you to maintain your success if you feel that you are ready. Or, if you are using the MiCBT practices, you can successfully determine when you are ready to progress to the next stage by regularly monitoring your improvements and assessing your approach.

Although you want to assess your approach on a regular basis, it is important that you do not assess it and consider it ineffective simply because you have not experienced immediate success. Be honest with yourself if you feel that you are using the best approach but that you need more time before you can experience full relief from your symptoms. Just because you are assessing your method does not mean that you need to change it, or that it is not working. It is simply an opportunity to reflect on your approach and ensure that you are taking the best one possible to support your healing process.

Integrating Supportive Practices

The supportive practices recommended in Part 4 of this book are not only highly valuable self-care practices but also have a very real impact on supporting your mental health. Integrating these practices into your life, in addition to maintaining your CBT approaches, is imperative if you want to experience consistent ongoing relief from your symptoms. You may find, in time, after your CBT approaches have successfully supported you in overcoming your anxious or depressive thoughts, that the supportive CBT practices are a great way to maintain your mental wellbeing. If you find yourself at this stage, incorporating these into your daily routine will ensure that you stay mentally healthy and that you reduce your vulnerability to experiencing difficult symptoms of anxiety or depression again.

As you integrate these supportive practices into your life, make sure that you are considering how they personally impact you. Remember, you are your primary focus here, so you need to always consider your thoughts and feelings when you are engaging in any behaviors that are intended to support your healing. Pick activities and self-care practices that genuinely fill you up and make you feel good about yourself. There is no shame in having a self-care game that looks completely different from how the "standard" self-care game looks or that it incorporates practices that were not listed above. As long as these practices are genuinely healthy for you and promote your mental (and physical) wellbeing in a positive manner, they are likely a great addition to your self-care routine. Keeping your routine personalized and productive will ensure that you do feel better when you engage in it and you can use this routine to support full relief from troubling emotional symptoms.

Any time you find yourself struggling to maintain your self-care practices, put extra effort in. Remember, depression and anxiety will encourage you to let basic self-care practices like eating a healthy meal and brushing your teeth seem like options instead of necessities. This is a false thought, and it needs to be replaced by engaging in healthier behaviors, such as actually eating a healthy meal and brushing your teeth. Even if your basic self-care practices are the only thing you have the energy to engage in all day long, put the effort in and make sure that you continue taking care of yourself. Not only do you deserve it, but you need it. Plus, these behaviors will help combat your depressive and anxious thoughts so that you can resume a healthier thinking pattern sooner.

Seeking Support When It's Needed

Just because you have made the decision to engage in self-healing does not mean you are immune to needing support. Support is an invaluable tool that can make your own self-healing practices far more effective and efficient. Learn how to ask for support when you need it and teach yourself how to find healthy support. This is a great way to help you experience greater success with CBT.

When you are seeking support, consider exactly what you need and make sure that you look in the right places for this support. For example, if you need support in processing difficult traumas from your past, consulting a friend may not be the best option. Although they mean well, your friend will likely not have the tools required to support you in the best way possible. Finding a professional therapist and letting them know that you are using a CBT approach is a great way to ensure that you get the support you need and that your therapy has the most powerful impact possible.

With that being said, do not discount the support of a positive friend who is compassionate and empathetic to you even when you are experiencing challenging emotions and thoughts. Friends and family members who show you compassion during your down times are invaluable and can support you by reminding you that you are loved and that you are worthy. If you are feeling anxious or depressed, you might feel compelled to isolate yourself from your loved ones and keep to yourself. You may experience cognitive distortions that tell you that they do not want to be around you or that you are a burden. Make sure that you use your CBT tools against these distortions to disprove them. Then, put as much effort as you feel you can into keeping your important relationships nurtured. If you are worried about being seen as a bad person for not being able to give as much energy or attention to your relationships, make sure that you stay transparent with your loved ones. Letting them know how you are feeling and being clear about the energy you have to contribute supports them in understanding you and can be extremely helpful in maintaining your relationships during troubling times.

Having Empathy for Yourself

It may seem hard at times, but having empathy for oneself is absolutely imperative. As you learned about with MiCBT, having empathy for yourself means that you give yourself the chance to remember that you are only human and that you are dealing with real and challenging problems. You are not required to be anything more than you are, and you are perfect as you are. Do not attempt to hold yourself to unreasonable standards or bully yourself because you feel that you are not producing the results that you desire. These types of behaviors are counterintuitive to your desired results and will prevent you from experiencing emotional resolve from things like anxiety, depression, anger, PTSD, and procrastination.

Being empathetic towards ourselves does not mean being complacent either. Your goal is not to let yourself off the hook for not taking positive action towards healing. Instead, it is to remind yourself that, sometimes, the results do not look as you wish they would and, sometimes, they take longer to achieve than you expected. This does not mean that you are a failure or that you are not worthy of healing. It simply means that you are having a hard time with your very real and very big emotions. Be gentle with yourself and express patience towards yourself when it comes to dealing with your emotions. The more patient and empathetic you are, the easier it will be for you to overcome your distressing feelings and find peace in your life.

Continually Educating Yourself

As someone who has dealt with psychological disorders, you are vulnerable to experiencing them again in your lifetime. Even if you experience complete relief from your CBT approach and you find yourself feeling much better, you may still find that your old behavioral cycles can be triggered from time to time. This happens because, in many cases, your old behavioral cycles have many different triggers. Each of which can be retriggered at any given time without any notice. During your CBT, you will encounter many of these triggers on a day-to-day basis and will overcome them using your CBT approaches. However, there may still be some triggers that you only encounter on an occasional basis rather than on a regular basis. As such, you may not get many chances to practice CBT on these triggers because you simply don't encounter them often enough. When this happens, if you are not careful, it can retrigger the occurrence of your depression or anxiety.

Continually staying educated on how you can lead a healthier mental life and assessing your thoughts for how they are supporting you is the best way to make sure that you are always equipped with the knowledge that you need to keep your mind healthy. Be sure to read up on mental health, stay focused on keeping your general health up, and educate yourself on the experiences that you may have if your depression, anxiety, PTSD, anger, or procrastination is retriggered. Regular education can help you stay clear on the warning signs and regain control over your mind before you experience a large problematic episode which can support you in staying clear of your disorder altogether.

Conclusion

You have completed reading *Cognitive Behavioral Therapy: An Essential CBT Guide to Rewiring the Brain and Overcoming Anxiety, Depression, and Intrusive Thoughts Using a Highly Effective Form of Psychotherapy*. The contents of this book should have supported you in understanding what CBT is and how it can support you in overcoming your psychological disorders and emotional symptoms.

Depending on how quickly you have read through this book, you may still be experiencing fairly intense symptoms of your emotional struggles despite having read everything within this book. It is important that you do not simply toss it aside and forget about it as you continue to face your daily struggles. Simply educating yourself on what needs to be done will not support you in healing. You will actually need to do the healing work. By remaining devoted and showing up for yourself every single day, you give yourself the attention that you need to truly embrace your healing journey with CBT.

It is important that you truly understand that self-healing does not mean isolating yourself from others. Isolating yourself is a common desire when you are experiencing something like anxiety or depression. However, doing so can impede your healing. Even on days where you do not feel like it, show up for yourself and attempt to make contact with at least one person per day who does not live with you. Doing so will support you in feeling a deeper sense of connection with those around you and will help you feel more attuned with the outside world.

You also need to make sure that you consistently practice your new mindfulness and CBT practices. Even though individuals who recover from psychological disorders using CBT are far less likely to relapse than those who are solely being treated with medicine, you will always be vulnerable to experiencing a relapse in your symptoms. Continuous self-monitoring and keeping yourself well-educated and equipped with the knowledge that you need to combat potential relapses will support you in overcoming them before they become problematic. Even if they do become problematic again, it is no reason to be ashamed.

Dealing with emotional disturbances like anxiety and depression is a real, valid, and often painful experience for anyone to endure. Be compassionate with yourself and trust that if you can treat yourself once, you can do it again. The more times you pick yourself back up, the harder it becomes for you to fall to the point of feeling irreparable.

As we wrap up, take a moment to consider how magnificent it is that you are here treating yourself. The amount of personal power that it takes for you to recognize that you are in need of support, and to have the willingness to step up and support yourself, and the amount of trust that you have placed in yourself and your ability – these are all admirable and goes to prove that you are a strong, capable, and worthy individual. You *can* heal from your emotions, and if you remain dedicated, you *will.*

When you put down this book, put it down knowing that it is always here, ready to be picked back up again at any time that you may need it. Rain or shine, 3:00 pm or 3:00 am, no matter where you are or who you are with, and no matter what you are feeling, this book is here for you as a constant resource to support you in overcoming any troubles you may be facing. If you simply need to reference this book for support or if you want to read it cover to cover once again, there is no right or wrong answer. No one will judge you if you feel that you need to re-educate yourself on the materials of this book so that you can continue moving towards your inner space of healing and freedom. Treat this book as your personal journal. It is a private and personal place for you to come to any time you need support or need to understand something within yourself on a deeper level.

If you enjoyed this book and felt that it added value to your life and supported you in truly overcoming your challenging emotional symptoms, please take the time to honestly review it on Amazon Kindle. If you know of someone else who may benefit from CBT, you may also consider letting them know about this book. The more that we can spread the message of healing and empower others to discover how they can heal themselves, the fewer people need to suffer from symptoms of anxiety and depression.